A Concrete Atlantis

A Concrete Atlantis

U.S. Industrial Building and
European Modern Architecture
1900–1925

Reyner Banham

The MIT Press
Cambridge, Massachusetts
London, England

This book was set in Gill Sans
by Achorn Graphic Services
and printed and bound by Halliday Lithograph
in the United States of America.

Library of Congress Cataloging-in-Publication Data
Banham, Reyner.
  A concrete Atlantis.

  Bibliography: p.
  Includes index.
  1. International style (Architecture)—Europe—American influences. 2. Architecture, Modern—20th century—Europe. 3. Industrial buildings—United States—Influence. 4. Concrete construction—United States. I. Title.
NA958.5.I58B36 1986   724.9'1   86-42
ISBN 0-262-02244-3

Dedicated to the memory of John Entenza and Nikolaus Pevsner, from both of whom I learned more than they ever taught me.

Acknowledgments   viii

Introduction   1

1   **The Daylight Factory**   23

2   **The Grain Elevator**   109

3   **Modernism and Americanism**   181

Notes   255

Index   261

Contents

Acknowledgments

A study such as this, which has taken me into many parts of the United States and some in Europe, leaves me deeply indebted to innumerable helpful persons and organizations, libraries, and other seats of learning: my prime debts to organizations are to the University of California, for a grant in aid of European travel and a timely sabbatical leave of absence; to the various libraries at the University of California at Berkeley and the McHenry Library at Santa Cruz; to the State University of New York at Buffalo and the students in the summer fieldwork sessions of 1977, 1978, and 1979; to Columbia University, students in the summer session of 1982, and the Avery Library; to the staff and library of the Historic American Engineering Record, Washington, D.C.; to the Library of the Royal Institute of British Architects; and to the Bartlett School of Architecture and Planning at University College London.

Individuals I will simply thank in alphabetical order and hope that I have overlooked none: A. Ardis Abbot, Bonnie Albert, John Allbright, Irving Amron, Jane Irene Atkinson, Patricia Layman Bazelon, Trevor Boddy, Kate Carroll, Charles D. Carter, John Carter, Melvin Charney, Will Clarkson, James Clifford, Carl Condit, Maria Grazia Dapra Conti, Emmy Dana, Frank Deni, Leonard K. Eaton, Robert M. Frame III, Angela Giral, members of the Gordon family, Dick

Graff, Morry Hoffman, Joe Hryvniak, Ada Louise Huxtable, Stuart Lacy, Randolph Langenbach, Bud Jacobs, Robert Kapsch, Carl Kessler, Daniel Kocieniewski, Kevin Mack, Tina Marenco, Joe Millar, Carol M. Morgan, Bruce Paul, Ron Perkins, Dale A. Peterson, Adolf K. Placzek, Jack Quinan, John D. Randall, Elisabeth Reidpath, Taina Rikala, Cervin Robinson, Joe Scalzo, Anatole Senkevitch Jr., Darrell A. Swanson, Donald Theurer, Tom Trotter, Nicholas Westbrook

. . . and all the janitors, security guards, engineers, receptionists, neighbors and others who arranged (above board, or below) for me to enter and study many more buildings than are mentioned in this text.

. . . the Great Atlantis (that you call America)

Introduction

This inquiry into the connections between North American industrial building and the classic modernist architecture of the International Style in Europe must cover many locations and publications on both sides of the Atlantic and might make its point of departure almost anywhere within its time span of 1900–1925; but the juncture at which its main currents seemed to spark together most enlighteningly in my own eyes was not in the presence of some monumental structure or provocative text, but among the abandoned onshore installations of the defunct sardine fisheries of Monterey Bay in California, almost the only point where this narrative intersects the main traditions of Western literature. In his picaresque novel *Cannery Row*, John Steinbeck, needing to explain a part of the tale's setting, gives a very plausible account of the disposal of some obsolete industrial equipment:

In April 1932 the boiler at the Hediondo Cannery blew a tube for the third time in two weeks and the board of directors consisting of Mr. Randolph and a stenographer decided that it would be cheaper to buy a new boiler than to have to shut down so often. In time the new boiler arrived and the old one was moved into the vacant lot between Lee Chong's and the Bear Flag Restaurant, where it was set up on blocks. . . . The boiler looked like an old-fashioned locomotive without wheels. It

had a big door in the center of its nose, and a low fire-door. . . .
Below the boiler on the hill there were a number of large pipes
also abandoned by the Hediondo.[1]

This makes an apt point at which to begin this study, not only because so much of the book will be about the abandoned installations of American industry—they are the preponderant subject of what might be called the observational parts, or fieldwork—or because the eyes that did the observing were my European ones, though this study is fundamentally concerned with European views of American industry, but also because of what occurred when I first started to visit Cannery Row in Monterey in the early 1980s.

In those days before the recent drastic "gentrifications," old-timers along the Row would still point out to unsuspecting tourists what they claimed were the original Hediondo "boilers and the big pipes where the hoboes used to sleep." The claim was false, however; the location did not tally with that clearly established in Steinbeck's text, any more than does the site of the present "boiler" that has been installed for the benefit of the organized tourist trade. More than that, Steinbeck also speaks of a single horizontal boiler, whereas what stood on this falsely identified site at the end of the Row were three tall, fat, crusty-black vertical cylinders that had probably once been oil tanks. Next to them, however—and this was what made the site so intriguing to me—was an apparently unfinished concrete structure, a flat, square ground-slab carrying one story-height of vertical square columns whose heads were joined by equally simple square concrete beams.[2] This was not great architecture, in the sense that many of the concrete-framed industrial buildings to be discussed later in this book are undoubtedly great by the standards of any period. Indeed it was barely architecture at all; it was like the merest diagram of an idealized reinforced concrete-frame structure, the sort of thing that used to appear in worthy books claiming to instruct lay-people in the fundamental principles of modern architecture, an image as familiar as any of the other older furniture of my mind.

But, looking through the open spaces defined by its square members to the closed bulks of the cylinders behind, I seemed to be seeing something else, equally familiar, but not observed in so perfectly abstracted a form before: the very essentials; the "ultimate metaphysic of form" of the high period of the International Style around 1930, as summed up in the "Two Geometries" of Le Corbusier; the "dialectical confrontation between sculptural forms and gridded space" of which Richard Etlin has spoken[3] and which I suggest is a European derivative of the closed forms of American industrial storage containers and of the openly gridded loft space of regular American factories.

This book will argue that there is a causal, cultural, and conscious connection between such masterworks of explicit architectural modernism as the Cité de Refuge or the Villa Savoye and the utilitarian structures of a certain period and type of North American industry. The existence of such a connection and its apparently deliberate nature have been noted from time to time in the literature of twentieth-century architecture. For instance, the authors of *Learning from Las Vegas* have observed:

The architecture of the Modern movement, during its early decades and through a number of its masters, developed a vocabulary of forms based on a variety of industrial models whose conventions and proportions were no less explicit than the Classical orders of the Renaissance. What Mies did with linear industrial buildings in the 1940s, Le Corbusier had done with plastic grain elevators in the 1920s, and Gropius had done with the Bauhaus in the 1930s (sic), imitating his own earlier factory, the Faguswerk of 1911. Their factorylike buildings were more than "influenced" by the industrial vernacular structures of the then recent past, in the sense that historians have described influences among artists and movements. Their buildings were explicitly adapted from these sources, and largely for their symbolic content, because industrial structures represented, for European architects, the brave new world of science and technology. . . .

Le Corbusier among the Modern masters was unique in elaborately describing industrial prototypes for his architecture in Vers une Architecture. However, even he claimed the steamship and the grain elevator for their forms rather than their associations, for their simple geometry rather than their industrial image. It is significant, on the other hand, that the buildings of Le Corbusier, illustrated in his book, physically resemble the steamships and the grain elevators but not the Parthenon or the furniture in Santa Maria in Cosmedin and Michelangelo's details for Saint Peter's, which are also illustrated for their simple geometric forms. The industrial prototypes became literal models for Modern architecture, while the historical-architectural prototypes were merely analogs selected for certain of their characteristics. To put it another way, the industrial buildings were the right style; the historical buildings were not.[4]

This was well observed (if somewhat self-contradictory and poorly argued), and the fundamental truth of its observations could be confirmed in almost daily confrontations and comparisons at any time after the International Style became the established mode for new constructions in North America. For a period at the end of the 1970s, for instance, one could look out over downtown Providence, Rhode Island, from the raised platforms of the train station and see the facade of a new multi-story hotel visually superimposed on that of an old, 1920s multi-story factory behind it—and the two facades were almost identical cellular grids of concrete structural members! Their dimensions and expression seemed the same, yet one had been built some forty years earlier than the other and for an entirely different stated function.

Now, one must acknowledge that there are accepted explanations for such resemblances that do not involve conscious emulation of forms. Many Marxist historians, as well as the kind of rationalist who used to offer the standard justifications for "modern architecture," would probably propose that the economic rationalities of society at those times would make that particular form of construction, with its necessary floor heights and structurally optimized bay widths between columns, the only conceivable mode of building

Concrete frame and abandoned tanks, Cannery Row, Monterey, California. (Photo, author)

Washburn-Crosby Elevator, Buffalo, as photographed by Erich Mendelsohn, 1924.

those structures, irrespective of their overt functions, since both were in practice conceived as little more than profitably rentable bulk floor space.

Such explanations may not be set aside; buildings in the "real world" are built for real-world reasons and will show the effects of those reasons and the world views that support them. Yet such explanations have nothing to say about the fact that profitably rentable hotel space of the same period as that factory did not exhibit its concrete frame in this way, but concealed it behind a garment of brick and stone in whatever period style was thought appropriate by architect and client. These simple economic explanations are not only too glib to explain what happened in detail, but also tend to look pitifully inadequate and subhuman when measured against the views and expressed responses of those "masters" whom *Learning from Las Vegas* credits with having imposed an industrial aesthetic on their architecture—Walter Gropius comparing American industrial buildings to the "work of the ancient Egyptians" in their overwhelming monumentality,[5] or Le Corbusier announcing that "The American engineers overwhelm with their calculations our expiring architecture,"[6] or Erich Mendelsohn in 1924 writing to his wife in Berlin after his visit to Buffalo, New York:

Mountainous silos, incredibly space-conscious, but creating space. A random confusion amidst the chaos of loading and unloading of corn ships, of railways and bridges, crane monsters with live gestures, hordes of silo cells in concrete, stone and glazed brick. Then suddenly a silo with administrative buildings, closed horizontal fronts against the stupendous verticals of fifty to a hundred cylinders, and all this in the sharp evening light.
I took photographs like mad. Everything else so far now seemed to have been shaped interim to my silo dreams. Everything else was merely a beginning.[7]

This kind of rhetoric seems to open up totally different types of historical questions, about the "why and wherefore" of the adoption of this industrial aesthetic, but these matters have been very little discussed in the literature so far. During the four decades when the International Style was the dominant architectural mode, such matters probably could not have been discussed at all. In the eyes of the great historians-apologists of the style, like Giedion and Pevsner, there would be little point in discussing what was a self-evident historical necessity. For them the International Style was not only the true style of the early twentieth century, as the Baroque had been of the late seventeenth, but was also a true style in the sense that, far from being copied from any previous epoch, it had arisen out of structural and constructional necessity, out of the service of the manifest needs of man and society, as the High Gothic of the thirteenth century was supposed to have done.

For that generation, the rationalist type of explanation was enough—or very nearly so. If the Bauhaus building looked like the Fagus factory, or the facades of Le Corbusier's *rues à Redents* looked somewhat like the elevations of Ford's Model-T plant at Highland Park, it was because all of these buildings were honest expressions of the functional needs of their users or inhabitants. At no time, one must suspect, was this kind of rhetoric believed absolutely; if Louis Sullivan's proposition that "form follows function" had been pursued objectively and resolutely, there would be no way in which a design school could look like a factory, or an apartment block in Paris could resemble an automobile plant in the Detroit suburbs. These doctrines and dictums, it now seems clear, were sincerely believed and honestly applied, but at the level of symbolism or (perhaps more accurately) as a form of allegory.

The appearance of industrial resemblances in nonindustrial buildings was construed, rather, as a *promise* that these buildings would be as functionally honest, structurally economical and, above all, as up-to-the-minute as any of the American factories that Le Corbusier hailed as "the first fruits of the New Age."[8] The forms of factories and grain elevators were an available iconography, a language of forms, whereby promises could be made, adherence to the modernist credo could be asserted, and the way pointed to some kind of technological utopia.

The word *utopia* is used advisedly but in a specialized sense here: it has become a commonplace that utopian dreams, utopian claims, utopian projects infest the architecture of the early years of the twentieth century and that modern technology was to play a large part in most of them. In this case, however, the utopia in view was not imaginary, improbable, nor located in the distant future. The industrial buildings of North America were distant from the younger European modernists only in mileage and were not imaginary; they had concrete—literally concrete—presence here on earth. European modernists may well have needed to make powerful imaginative leaps in order to comprehend what they believed to be happening in North America, and the views they expressed may have been flavored by their own wishful imaginings, but unlike other utopians they could point to an apparently ideal state of affairs that actually existed in their own time. That is why I have chosen to call it an *Atlantis* rather than a *utopia,* taking my cue from Francis Bacon's "New Atlantis," in which he describes an island in the ocean some long way to the west of Europe and specifically compares it to "the Great Atlantis (that you call America)," though only to differentiate the real place from the imaginary.[9]

However, Bacon's Atlantis suggests even richer comparisons with what was happening in the minds of European modernists who turned to American industrial architecture for inspiration. His New Atlantis was a society transformed by the application of scientific method, but on almost every page of the text one is made aware of the extent to which its continued functioning was governed by the persistence of rules of conduct based on Christian charity and Christian grace. The idealized but concrete industrial architecture of North America, the product of a strict and modern engineering rationalism derived from the kind of scientific methodology proposed by Bacon, was also discovered to contain the perennial and absolute virtues of an earlier architectural tradition: Le Corbusier believed that the work of these engineers rang "in unison with universal order,"[10] while Walter Gropius more pointedly supposed that "American builders have preserved a natural feeling for large compact forms fresh and intact."[11]

One may find these views naive, but they contain concepts and understandings shot through with the cultural contradictions of the world of architecture in the first decades of the present century: that simultaneous quest for pure modernity and also ancient certainty that informs the works, and above all the writings, of Adolf Loos, for example. Loos was also one of the key figures in establishing the period's pervasive myths of the clean modernity of America.[12] In the context of European understandings of industrial architecture, however, these generalized ideas take on a sharper point. America was not only the land of the future, as generations of hopeful Europeans had supposed, but was also—and here again it is Gropius who produces the telling phrase—the *Mutterland der Industrie.*

If the interests and researches of that generation had been more rational and less romantic, the European modernists could have found nearly all the virtues and architectural forms they admired in America among the works of their direct European predecessors; indeed many of the American concrete structures they celebrated would have been impossible without the patented processes and the built examples of European engineers. But America had an overwhelming and legendary prestige for modernity—and many of the European engineers would be compromised, in the eyes of younger, radical architects, by their association with established architects of the older, unreformed and nonmodern generation. Even so, it seems to be true in the end that it was only some kind of chapter of fortunate accidents in architectural patronage and periodical publication that finally gave America the special status of the Concrete Atlantis.

Architecture remains a predominantly visual art; this may be regrettable but it is a historical and cultural fact, and it means that architects are educated and influenced primarily by the force of visual example. What were the most fundamental examples for this particular group is abundantly clear:

Elevators on the Buffalo River; view
downstream from South Street.
(Photo, Patricia Layman Bazelon)

Grain elevators, sketches by Erich
Mendelsohn, 1914–15.

seven pages of almost unexplained illustrations of American grain elevators and factories that appeared as an insert in the *Jarhbuch des Deutschen Werkbundes* for 1913. These illustrations immediately followed an important introductory article by the Werkbund's president Friedrich Naumann[13] and were thus also the first illustrations seen by the reader. But they belonged to the following article, "Die Entwicklung Moderner Industriebaukunst," by Walter Gropius, who had been soliciting these pictures from various sources in America and Canada for over a year during the preparation of the article. What had specifically turned his attention to American industrial building, however, cannot have been direct experience, since he was not to cross the Atlantic until after he left the Bauhaus in 1928. It must have been his connections with the Benscheidt family in Hannover and Alfeld, who were his clients on the Fagus factory. They had seen American plants in 1910 during their meetings with the United Shoe Machinery Company in Beverly, Massachusetts, the firm who was the prime investor in the Fagus concern and whose Beverly factory, designed by the great concrete "pioneer" Ernest L. Ransome, was a model demonstration structure in the most up-to-date mode.

The impact of these illustrations, however, was felt throughout "modern Europe" and registered as early as 1914 in the work of Antonio Sant'Elia and Mario Chiattone, the architect members of the Futurist circle in Italy, and even more strikingly in the sketchbooks and imaginary projects of Erich Mendelsohn—these indeed were the preliminary outlines of the "silo dreams" that were realized before his eyes in Buffalo in 1924. In 1919 Le Corbusier (who was not to set foot in any America for another sixteen years) wrote to Gropius asking to borrow the grain elevator illustrations for use in the magazine *L'Esprit Nouveau*,[14] and a year later one of them appeared in an article by Erich Mendelsohn. By 1927, when two of Gropius's illustrations appeared in *Der Sieg des Neuen Baustils* by Walter Curt Behrendt,[15] they had already become almost commonplace, having been seen worldwide in the book *Vers une Architecture,* which Le Corbusier assembled out of those earlier

Elevators and factories presented by
Walter Gropius in *Jahrbuch des
Deutschen Werkbundes*, 1913.
(Courtesy Avery Library, Columbia
University)

Grain silo and elevator, Fort William

Grain silo, Bunge y Born,
Buenos Aires

Corn silo, South America

Continental Motor Manufacturing
Company, Detroit, Michigan

Alling and Corry, Cincinnati

U.S. Printing Company, Cincinnati

magazine articles. From then on, they were established icons of modernity and architectural probity. Their last appearance without satire or historicizing commentary was, as far as one can tell, in Vincent Scully's *American Architecture and Urbanism* in 1969.[16]

How could fourteen illustrations, only moderately well reproduced from other publications, ever attain such commanding and durable power? For a start, the practitioners of the International Style—then innocently known as just "modern architecture"—needed objective confirmation of their formal preferences. Believing itself to be the very antithesis of a revived or invented style, the movement had to take a stand somewhere outside the "fevered imaginations of architects" or the supposedly hot-house atmosphere of the academies. "Let us believe the words of American engineers," said Le Corbusier, "but let us beware of American architects!"[17] This command will need further attention in the last section of this book, but here it serves to indicate a state of mind that sought architectural virtue by going outside the privileged circles of professional architecture as then understood, much as previous generations with similar problems had turned to the vernacular buildings of peasants and primitives in search of honest constructions and clear expressions of function.

In an age when pretensions of peasant primitivism were becoming increasingly difficult for a sophisticated person to sustain (if only because peasant standards of personal hygiene were no longer tolerable to sensitive souls in Europe), works of engineering were happily co-opted as manifestations of a kind of modern "noble savagery" compatible with twentieth-century styles of life, and could be held up as models for emulation.

At stake here may be a larger issue, with broader cultural resonances. Vague or tentative connections between "primitivism" and matters mechanical were fairly generally felt in the avant-garde culture of Europe in the early twenties, especially in Paris, and even more especially in attitudes to jazz music. Jazz clearly interested everybody, including Le Corbusier; and while it may not be literally true that

Josephine Baker meant as much to him as grain elevators, she may have meant something similar. Jazz, it would seem, could be regarded as primitively African, in spite of the fact that it came to Paris from North America, but its rhythms—loud, persistent to the point of monotony, and *ostinato*—agreed pretty well with what many avant-garde artists of the time believed to be the rhythms of machinery.

A suggestively complex case in point, from circles close to Le Corbusier, would be the ballet *La Création du monde*, with jazz-inspired music by Darius Milhaud and scenery by Fernand Léger. The latter, while patently and even eruditely inspired by the African art he had sketched in museums, expressed, according to Léger himself, the idea that man is a mechanism like everything else. Beyond that, many of the forms and colors he used in this primitive/mechanical setting seem very close kin to the forms and colors he is known to have admired in mass-produced entertainment art, modern advertising, and automobiles and aircraft. These connections were obviously based on fashion and sentiment, not learning or logic, but by their very ambiguities they provided a rich mixture—out of which the idea of engineering as a form of modern noble savagery could grow—whose homeland, like that of savage/mechanical jazz, could be identified as North America.

These ambiguities, and a general lack of systematic knowledge of the materials under review, freed aesthetes and architects to pick and choose the objects they felt to be truly primitive or properly mechanistic and thus to reject some types of perfectly valid structural procedures, for instance, as corruptions of what they felt to be the true forms of unspoiled engineering. Fundamental aesthetic preferences could still override even the supposedly unquestionable authority that came with the "objectivity" of engineering design.

So not all works of engineering were indiscriminately admired: the rectangular grids of American factories and the closed cylinders of grain elevators were acceptable, but other types of engineering structures did not suit all modern tastes. The diagonal lattices and tapering trusses of bridges and cranes were unacceptable in some modern Parisian quarters. "The work of the engineer, pure in its origins, begins gradually to be adulterated by aesthetic pursuits. The crane which is seen on this page is soaked in romantic expressionism," averred an anonymous caption writer in *Cahiers d'Art* in 1926 under an illustration of a spidery but otherwise ordinary German coaling gantry.[18] The comment is the more remarkable since it is perfectly obvious to us now, and must have been equally so then to thoughtful observers, that neither the designers nor the investors in such an installation would be likely to deviate from the strict and objective rationality of economical construction—or profit, if you prefer.

The selective attitude toward the authority of rational industrial structures has an inverted corollary in the architects' attitudes toward one of the most notorious of all topics in the discussion of their architecture, the flat roof. One could reasonably propose that the flat roof became one of the consciously selected symbols of their modernity; and at the highest levels of architectural discourse, the question of flat versus pitched roofs is purely—but explosively—an aesthetic or cultural matter. At a more mundane level, however, such discourse is prone to descend to the simple asseveration that "everybody knows that flat roofs leak!"

If, as now seems likely and will be argued here, the preferred flat-roofed silhouettes of the International Style derived to some significant degree from the fact that the American industrial buildings they knew from pictures had flat roofs more often than not, then an interesting question is deflected back to the builders of those American factories and warehouses: How could they be so suicidally perverse as to prefer a roof form that contradicted the norms of rationality, economy, and profitability by leaking? And why did the European modernists copy a feature that was, apparently, so unfunctional? Why, in rejecting the splayed lattice legs of the coaling gantry, did they spurn a functional and economical form of construction, while accepting, in the flat roof, a form that was neither?

The answer is that while European flat roofs may indeed have leaked as often as was claimed, the American industrial ones generally did not, and some that I have examined still do not, eighty or more years after their construction. A properly detailed and constructed flat roof can be as stanch as any pitched roof. The actual failure rate of flat roofs in Europe is debatable, and has been much debated.[19] Success in building them, even in rainier northern European climates, dates to several decades before 1900 and thus well before the onset of modernism. If the modernist versions leaked, they must have had some source outside local, current, and commonsense building practices.

This was indeed the case; too many of them were purely formalistic imitations of structures that had never been studied firsthand. Their designers had not seen the originals and had no opportunity to examine and understand how they should be designed, detailed, and constructed. And this brings up a matter of extraordinary historical importance that goes well beyond any scandals about leaking roofs: insofar as the International Style was copied from American industrial prototypes and models, it must be the first architectural movement in the history of the art based almost exclusively on photographic evidence rather than on the ancient and previously unavoidable techniques of personal inspection and measured drawing.

It could, however, be argued that this was entirely appropriate because the power of the photographs comes from the fact that, like the works of engineering they represented, they were understood to be the product of the scientific application of natural laws. Having come into the hands of their European admirers in the guise of news photographs, rather than that of "art" photography, they were supposedly free from those elements of personal selection and interpretation that must inevitably infect any artistic rendering, or even the traditional production by architectural draftsmen of finished drawings from measured field notes. The photographs represented a truth as apparently objective and modern as that of the functional structures they portrayed.

That, obviously, would be one source of their strength in the eyes of a generation that sought certainty in architecture; but such power to convince usually derives from two other factors: the nature of the objects represented and the expectations of those that look upon those representations. The young radicals of modern Europe clearly believed that they saw here the work of minds as radical as their own; but was this indeed the case? The main burden of this study will be to examine the buildings in question in a way that was not available to Gropius in 1913: firsthand and—as was my good fortune—on the basis of daily familiarity, and with access to the history of the developments that had given them the forms they presented to European eyes. For the American buildings were hardly radical or innovative in the ways that were often supposed; and on closer study the factories, at least, can be seen as the end products of a building tradition whose sources were firmly struck in Europe itself and reached back as far as the later Middle Ages, to the great warehouses of the Hanseatic ports and other multi-story structures for trade and, later, manufacturing industry. And these great factories were the very end of that tradition, a doomed building type, which, by the time it was taken up in Europe and before Mendelsohn set foot in Buffalo or Detroit, had already ceased to be modern enough to satisfy the needs of innovative American industry.

They were, however, buildings of great quality and power. They were as good as their European admirers had supposed, and one must wonder by what process of photographic divination they managed to recognize these qualities in buildings they had never seen. It is not enough to say that some aspects of these industrial structures chimed in with their aesthetic or stylistic preferences, though it is startling to see how truthful and powerful were, say, Mendelsohn's early and impressionistic sketches of these buildings he had never seen. Aesthetic predisposition may be enough to account for their immediate impact on that generation, but it is not enough when one stands in front of the buildings themselves. They do have an almost Egyptian monumentality in many cases, and in abandonment and death they evoke the majesties of a departed civilization. Or so it used to seem to me, looking downstream on the Buffalo River from the angle of South Street. On either side of the water, like an avenue of mighty tombs, were structures representing almost the whole history of the grain elevator; certainly, no other city in the world possessed so concentrated a set of historically valuable elevators as Buffalo then did, along that half mile of river down to the Ohio Street Bridge. It was a privilege to know them in their ravaged antique grandeur, just as it was to work in Buffalo, for however short a period, in a classic and sophisticated example of a "Daylight" factory. Whatever the shortcomings of its antique heating system and ill-used windows that blew open during blizzards and filled my office with snow, the factory's columned interior had a grave pre-Classical regularity that did indeed look as if it might contain some ancient secret law of great architecture.

I was moved by these buildings, and that was partly because I came upon them unprepared. They were as unknown to me as they must be to any student or lover of architecture because, outside the modernists' polemics of the twenties, they have practically no part in the records of architectural history and have yet to draw a critic worthy of their austere virtues. That is regrettable, for they deserve a better fate than to be left to the industrial archaeologists and prettifying rehabilitators who seem at present to be the only parties with any interest in them. They need to be brought back among "the canons of giant architecture," and they deserve far more respect and honor than they commonly receive in America, for—as much as the work of a Richardson or a Wright—they represent the triumph of what is American in American building art.

They also represent one of the earliest and most powerful influences of American building art on the rest of the world. The impact of H. H. Richardson or Frank Lloyd Wright, for instance, has been extensively studied and documented because they were acknowledged to be great architects and were expected to affect the work of other creative talents. The factories and grain elevators, however, seem to have been influential precisely because they were thought to derive from some subculture that did not normally connect to the high culture of architects and other artists. And, insofar as these supposedly nonarchitectural industrial buildings may have helped to fix the forms and usages of what we now call "The International Style," which has so far been the dominant style of twentieth-century architecture, Americans owe them the same degree of respect they award other native arts that have affected the rest of the world, such as the Hollywood film, dance theater, and jazz.

Ultimately, however, our study must return to the European modernists themselves. They were the ones who made the International Style international and finally brought it back to North America in the thirties. Furthermore, it was they who had set up the categories and attitudes with which I—a well-trained child of their modern movement but an uninformed stranger—came to the Concrete Atlantis and was moved by its monuments. Any search for an understanding of why those factories and elevators look so good to us now must also involve some attempt to understand the ambitions, expectations, and frame of mind that drove the founding fathers of the modern movement to adopt these monuments as the models for their new architecture—which was also, somehow, expected to rediscover and then embody the eternal and fundamental verities underlying all great architecture, old as well as new.

No more striking testimony of this paradoxical mind-set can be found than the text with which this book concludes: Edoardo Persico's encomium on the Fiat factory in Turin. Familiar with its interior operations as a daily employee but apparently unaware that it was designed in deliberate imitation of an American factory (since he never mentions the fact), he nevertheless finds in it intimations of order, even a divine order like that of the Gothic cathedrals. In this building that was to become a *locus classicus* of modernism and a place of pilgrimage for modernists, who liked to have themselves photographed on its rooftop racetrack as proof that they were indeed *moderner Menschen,* Persico found, among its concrete columns and under the stare of its enormous windows, compelling evidence of "an ancient order of . . . obedience to the Laws."

*Pure, clear, uncolored daylight—the sunshine of roofless fields
. . . is becoming the possession of the American factory laborer.*

The American Architect and Building News, 1911

I

The Daylight Factory

Bethune Hall

In its best years, toward the end of the 1970s, the School of Architecture and Environmental Design of the State University of New York at Buffalo occupied a building whose main known claim to historical fame was that it had been named Bethune Hall by the university, in honor of Louise Blanchard Bethune, Buffalo's first known woman architect. This dedication was a characteristic piece of liberal pietism of the times, no doubt intended as official prophylaxis against the feminist wraths to come. Its interest for me, however, was less in this historical transvestism than in a powerful sense of *déja vu* that gripped me on my very first encounter with it.

As the dean's car turned into the potholed driveway that ran along the flank of the building, I found myself looking at a structure that appeared to have escaped from the pages of the second "Rappel à MM. les Architectes" in Le Corbusier's best-known book, *Vers une Architecture*. In fact, it was not one of the buildings that illustrated the "Reminder to Architects" about the "generating and accusing lines" that animate a building's surface and give it individuality.[1]

It was, however, a structure of the same type and generation as those Le Corbusier had used to exemplify his arguments: multi-story American industrial buildings with exposed concrete frames, filled in only by transparent glazing; buildings like X-ray images, their very bones on public

Bethune Hall (formerly Buffalo Meter Company), Buffalo, New York, by Lockwood, Greene and Co., 1915–17. (Photo, Bazelon)

Bethune Hall, pilaster and cornice at
corner of block. (Photo, Bazelon)

Bethune Hall, interior, May 1977.
(Photo, author)

display. Bethune Hall was immediately identifiable as being of that typology. It stood four stories tall and four bays wide by twelve bays long; and every bay of its tidily exposed reinforced concrete frame was filled entirely with glass carried in standard steel sash, but for a shallow spandrel or apron of red brick below the sill. The roof was almost flat, behind a slight cornice; an attic set back from the perimeter was also flat-roofed. Everything was neat, rectangular, rational, and self-assured, as my readings in Le Corbusier had suggested it would be! But instead of looking at a badly rescreened reproduction in his book, I was facing the real thing, and it was good. The first glimmerings of a book on the Concrete Atlantis began to glow in my mind at that point.

Strictly speaking, I was not looking at quite the genuine Corbusian article. What can be seen grimly in his illustrations are buildings of stunning simplicity and brutal crudity, elementary rectangular grids of plain rectangular members, diagrammatic and reductionist, undoubtedly for compelling economic reasons. Bethune Hall, on closer examination, was less flatly basic than that, as daily familiarity and the close studies of my students made increasingly clear. It had subtleties, airs, and graces, some of which Le Corbusier might have despised. High up under the cornice on each of the corner piers, for instance, was a decorative label in a style something between drastically simplified Louis Sullivan and an anticipation of post-Cubist Art Deco. Could it possibly be a structural refinement of some sort, or was it what it appeared to be, a decorative device, the ghost, as it were, of the garlands of fruit and flowers that had drooped below the capitals of ornate pilasters in the gaudier late forms of Beaux-Arts classicism?

Similarly, was the fact that the pilasters at the corners were wider than the regular piers along the facade a contribution to the stability of the structure against side loads, or did they simply echo the double-pilaster stops and other forms of emphasis that had customarily closed the ends of the long, repetitive columniations of classical facades ever since Bramante's so-called House of Raphael? And that cornice above: though drawings in the university's files showed that it had been ingeniously designed to keep rainwater clear of the facade, they also confirmed what the eye saw from below—moldings simplified from classical prototypes. The way the cornice turned the corner above those broader pilasters also seemed to raise some interesting questions. It was not a simple right-angled turn, but was notched by a double reentrant, echoing with proper classicist discipline the similar double reentrant between the edges of the two pilasters below.

Historically, this was most provoking. It seemed to demand for Bethune Hall a place, not in the archives of industrial archaeology, but in the history of architecture—somewhere between Bramante, the likely inventor of the double-reentrant device at corners, and Mies van der Rohe, who was to produce a similar kind of refinement, but in steel, for the corners of his buildings on the IIT campus in the 1950s. Further apparent anticipations of Mies could be seen in the plan of Bethune Hall, whose empty rectangularity, whose universal, indifferent industrial loft space, interrupted only by columns at eighteen-foot centers on a square grid, was partitioned by a solid block (packed with services and communications) rising through all four floors and dividing the simple rectangular layout into unequal but proportional "halves."

Internally, it presented an equally confusing but captivating aspect. On the floors that the architecture school occupied, all surfaces but the floor (which was now carpeted) had been stripped, scrubbed, purged of industrial dirt and all signs of previous history, and, in general, painted white. Although much academic furniture and drawing equipment had been moved in, rather frequent changes of curricular dispositions meant that large areas might be totally cleared of furnishings at times and the bare geometry of the structure revealed for a space of several bays. It was an ideal space in many senses of the word: ideal for the environmental needs and purposes of an architecture school as then generally understood; ideal as a demonstration of the basic preferences—spare, clean, well lit, undecorated, and so forth—of the established tradition of modern architecture; and ideal also in the more mystical sense of demonstrating the *Idea dell'Architettura* as the Italian "rigorists" of the eighteenth century would have understood it, the fundamental system of horizontals and verticals, loads and supports, spaced in the most rational and economical manner discoverable. It was the basic structural imagery to which the so-called rationalist tradition has had recourse ever since its foundation—which, it sometimes seems to be implied, must have been at the very beginning of architectural time!

It was also extremely beautiful in its white purity when it was empty; but the system of construction then revealed was not in fact the ideal diagram of columns and beams that Le Corbusier clearly had in mind—and that so many American factories do indeed exhibit. Bethune Hall's columns were not square but octagonal; their tops flared in a gentle curve to almost twice the section of the straight shaft below and supported a flat floor slab above, without beams or joists. Only at the perimeter was this variation on "mushroom construction" replaced by anything closer to post-and-beam construction; there neat triangular shear brackets transferred the floor loads to the backs of the square external columns.

These usages have a particular historical interest, as I was later to discover: the use of different "systems" or even "orders" for the internal and external columns would have struck many rationalists and younger architectural radicals as illogical or even improper, since it multiplied the number of different types of components in the frame. Against this one could argue something that many a promoter of ideal, rational constructional systems has had to concede when practicality is required: the conditions of an exposed external column loaded on only three sides and of an even more exposed corner column loaded on only two are radically different from those of a symmetrically loaded internal column protected from the elements. There may be good and rational reasons for handling exterior columns differently; equally, however, there could also be a local tradition of American industrial construction working here, with attitudes left over from the days before concrete frames, when the masonry exteriors of mills and factories and their wooden internal structures were indeed two very different things. As we shall see, even some of the inventors of the true concrete frame were slow to see that external columns could be the same as internal ones.

If I seemed to be looking at a surviving traditionalism when I compared the external columns with those of the interior, there was no doubt that the latter represented the party of rational progress. Their mildly flared capitals seem to have been an experiment (the drawings, again, showed two different and uncommon arrangements of the reinforcement inside the columns), possibly as an attempt to get away from the already classic format of the mushroom-and-slab form of construction, by then established for barely a decade in Europe by Robert Maillart and independently in the United States by Charles Turner of Minneapolis.

The adventurous, sophisticated, but remarkably simple-looking form of construction at Bethune Hall should be noted and carefully pondered. It renders impossible the kind of stylistic judgment that might be easily made by someone, like me, with a regular art-historical training and a modernist background: that this not-quite-modern-looking building with its occasional reminiscences of an older, decorated architecture, but with a very up-to-date interior represented some kind of pure, stripped modernism "struggling to be born out of the cocoon of the past."

Far from representing an emergent style, in the early stages of the art-historian's unquestioned cycle of primitive/mature/decadent, Bethune Hall's architecture presented what Le Corbusier would have called a style "en pleine décadence," well past its maturity and only a few steps from oblivion. The type of factory building that is exemplified in Bethune Hall, the "Daylight" factory, may have been almost two centuries in the coming, as I shall suggest, but in its classic, concrete-framed form it had emerged only in 1903 and had reached a startling and precocious maturity by 1910 or 1911. By the time Bethune Hall was designed for the old Buffalo Meter Company, the Daylight factory was on the point of being replaced by a new and even more radical type of factory, the single-story, steel-framed workshed. In apostrophizing the concrete-framed factory as some kind of perennial ideal, Le Corbusier, and Walter Gropius before him, had chosen a building type that was already proving to be but a short interlude in the history of American industrial building, however permanent the monuments it may have left behind.

Because these structures were so well made, many of them have survived to show what a sound, if misconstrued, choice the European modernists made in selecting them as their models. The best of them are superb examples of engineering intelligence and the designer's craft, and, for all those who respect good architecture, they are important as sound, functional, and sometimes very moving examples of the "fine art of building." They have the Vitruvian virtues of *firmness,* since they still stand; *commodiousness,* since they have proven highly adaptable to new uses after their first functions have disappeared; and *delight,* since they can still generate those mysterious emotions and responses that are supposed to be the prerogative of great architecture.

In the year that I worked in Bethune Hall, I came to feel this ever more strongly, as my acquaintance with the building grew and my research uncovered more information about it. The campus files produced not only drawings of the building's details and plan, but also the fact that it had been commissioned by the Buffalo Meter Company, who moved into it in 1917. They had been model employers in the heyday of Buffalo's industrial greatness; the proprietor, who still lived as a very old man only a few blocks away, had insisted that, over and above the general system of heating by steam, there should also be open-fronted gas fires in the work spaces, placed close to the entrances, where employees could dry their boots and socks after trudging to work through the snow that is Buffalo's lot for some four months every year.

That was gossip-information; what came from the drawings was the existence of an alternative arrangement for the reinforcing in the columns, with four angle-irons back to back instead of the much more conventional ring of vertical rods, spirally bound around the outside, that was in the built version. And from the drawings, too, came the confirmation that the elegant subdivision of the plan by the cross-block containing all the toilets, stairs, elevators, and services was aboriginal, so to speak, a part of the primary design concept and not a later rationalization of an excessively unspecific plan. I also learned the name of the designers and engineers: the Boston firm of Lockwood, Greene and Co., an omni-competent office that could undertake every stage in setting up a new industrial plant from selecting the site to installing the machinery. Although Lockwood, Greene and Co. are now headquartered in New York and do not quite dominate the business as they did at the turn of the century, they were indeed one of the biggest names in American industrial architecture for decade after decade, and their works proved to be a very large part, sometimes the very best part, of the buildings I found myself studying when I finally committed myself to the writing of the present book.

Among the many things for which I am indebted to Bethune Hall is that it introduced me to my subject matter somewhere near the very top in quality. But chiefly I am in-debted to it for also introducing me to the very considerable ambiguities of the history of which it forms part; for alerting me to the fact that this history would not be a simple linear progression, rational innovation by rational innovation, from inadequate and wasteful older types of buildings to the kind of clean, well-lighted places that the modernists of Europe believed they were admiring. There would prove to be few radical breaks or flashes of startling originality; rather, it had been a cautious and none-too-precipitate advance into the world of concrete framing and total daylighting. For good and unforgiving economic reasons, it was an advance that had to avoid rash and potentially expensive innovations, and, not surprisingly, some major developments were achieved almost it seems by accident, or under the impression that something quite different was being achieved.

Ransome and the Former Tradition
The seemingly serendipitous process leading to the invention of the concrete-framed factory—almost a "sleepwalker's" approach, in Arthur Koestler's useful phrase—is best shown

in the work of Ernest L. Ransome, possibly one of the greatest of all the concrete pioneers of the later nineteenth century. He is the apparent inventor of the concrete frame in its American version and thus of the true Daylight factory—though he was an unconscionable time getting to it. Born in 1852, Ransome was descended from the Ransomes of Ipswich, a distinguished English dynasty of ironfounders and engineers, who left a worldwide mark on products as diverse as road rollers, lawn mowers, and (in their Ransome-and-Marles incarnation) ball bearings. Although the family business was metallurgical, Ernest's father was also interested in the production of artificial stones, including artificial grinding stones, and finally came up with a form of cement which he attempted to market in the United States. I have seen trade literature produced by him out of Baltimore in the 1860s,[2] and it appears that the young Ernest crossed the Atlantic shortly after that to help with the business.

He turned up in California in the seventies; and if he went there, as is reported, hoping to market a cement-block construction system of earthquake-resisting specification, he seems to have abandoned this presumably self-frustrating project by the early eighties, when he appeared as an advocate of reinforced construction in monolithic poured concrete. As a practical building-site technique, reinforcement was still in a crude and improvisatory phase of development (Ransome used scrap railroad rails on occasion) and there was plenty of scope for experiment. His energy, inventiveness, and, above all, the astuteness and speed with which his slightest invention was immediately locked up in secure patents, have ensured him a permanent place in the annals of concrete construction, but for reasons that too often do him less than justice as a constructor.

During the earlier phases of the writing of the history of modern architecture, down to about 1940, when authors tended to emphasize the pioneering use of "new" materials like cast iron, glass, steel, and concrete, any engineer or architect who availed himself of any of these at an early enough date, however dim or dubious the actual work done with it, was apparently assured of an honored place in the modernist pantheon. Ransome, therefore, is sometimes brought forward as an important pioneer by historians who, I regret to say, seem to have no idea of what any of his works look like. Furthermore, the extensive repertory of patents has provided a rich lode of documentation for the bibliographic type of historian to excavate and then reconstruct as an impressive apparatus of footnotes, again at the expense of studying the work. Between these two approaches, much of Ransome's early work, particularly in California, has disappeared without being historically recorded or properly studied.

Fortunately, however, two small underpass bridges from his drawing board survive in Golden Gate Park in San Francisco. One of them bears the commemorative plaque of a National Historic Civil Engineering Landmark—as indeed it should since the bridges were built in 1886–87 and are therefore the first reinforced-concrete bridges in North America and among the first three or four in the entire world, as far as can be judged. Although not directly relevant to the present study, these bridges are highly instructive in showing the attitude with which Ransome appears to have entered the business of design. These were works of "civil architecture" not "industrial building" and were therefore decorated, as the civic customs of the period would expect, with sub-historical detailing of the type fancied in California at that time.

That decoration, which seems to aspire to the Eastlake/ Queen Anne mode, is in no way derived from the nature of the material employed, but generally imitates stonework practices, or even carpentry. What the appearance of the bridges does derive from the particular constructional technology employed is that in places the surface of the concrete is overprinted with the grain pattern and the jointing of the wooden form against which the concrete was cast. In general, Ransome's work of this and later periods, while innovative in technique, is not often radical in architectural conception or in the choice of style, though in this matter he was often at the mercy of the architects of title for the design (Julia Morgan at Mills College, for instance, or Percy and Hamilton at Stanford University). Even so, it seems doubtful, as one surveys his total output, whether this would have troubled his conscience as a designer: he probably found it quite proper that the niceties and decencies of his time, class, and provincial environment should be observed.

In a drastically simplified way, the same sort of nicety persists throughout his work as an industrial architect as well. If the Weed/McNear warehouse in Port Costa, California is indeed the slightly mysterious building at "Wheatport" mentioned by Carl Condit in *American Building Art,*[3] then it is the earliest surviving work by Ransome for an industrial use and possibly the earliest concrete industrial building in the United States. Its interest here, however, is less its early date than the style in which it is presented. Poured concrete is used to form the outer wall of a structure otherwise conventionally constructed with internal wooden columns, beams, and floors. Concrete has simply replaced the brick or stone outer walls of the former tradition, and significant details (insofar as so elementary a building can be said to be detailed) effectively confirm this.

All the door and window openings on the street facade, for instance, have segmentally arched tops—a usage that is quite gratuitous in reinforced concrete, which need not be arched for strength across an opening because its steel reinforcement can accept the tensional load in the bottom of a flat beam, whereas a similar span in masonry or brick construction would have to be arched in order to avoid tension in its lower chord. A flat beam requires much simpler and cheaper formwork than even the plainest type of arch. Ransome, if it was he, seems unwilling to make a break against visual custom, even when it is uneconomical. This kind of cultural timidity would not be unexpected in a provincial work of a transitional type, but it was a personal trademark of Ransome's until well after 1900.

It was so much a trademark, indeed, that it was what set me to wondering if this might be a Ransome design. Stylistic connoisseurship of such very primitive buildings is a risky business, but I have to say that the type of window and the mix of the concrete, especially the type of aggregate, make

this look like a Ransome building to me. Both the style of window opening and the type of aggregate were to reappear as late as the United Shoe Machinery plant, for instance; and the same sort of aggregate, with its small, sharp, triangular stones, appears in other works attributed to Ransome.

The segmentally arched window openings, and other usages inherited from the former tradition, were very visibly employed in his other industrial Californian works of the eighties and the nineties, though we have to rely on photographic evidence for this because all the major and securely attributed works have been demolished for some time now. Of these, the two most consequential were the Arctic Oil Company building, on the China Basin in San Francisco, and the Pacific Coast Borax Company depot, on a waterside site inside the perimeter fence of what is now the U.S. Navy base at Alameda. They were sufficiently alike to suggest that there was a Ransome office style in the nineties, at least: both were multi-storied clerestory sheds of similar profile, presenting the gables of their pitched roofs on their narrow ends. Their style can best be called negligent-classical. Ransome seems to dispose of a number of simplified classical devices such as cornices and brackets, which he uses in an *ad hoc* kind of way, without discipline or apparent knowledge of

Arctic Oil Works, San Francisco,
California (destroyed), by Ernest L.
Ransome, 1884. (From *Reinforced
Concrete Buildings,* 1912)

Pacific Coast Borax Company,
Alameda, California (destroyed), by
Ernest L. Ransome, 1888–89. (From
*Reinforced Concrete in Factory Con-
struction,* 1907)

Buffalo Weaving Company plant,
Buffalo, New York, 1889–95.
(Photo, Bazelon)

their proper deployment, and only when it is reasonably economical to do so. Nevertheless the segmentally arched window persists and in a way that underlines its ultimate extraction from the kind of Georgian buildings that Ransome would have known in his youth. The windows are still seen as openings made in a wall, and the wall is horizontally grooved to represent rustication, both in these large Californian works and in the first industrial plants he put up in the eastern states.

The true construction of this imitation rusticated wall, where it survives to be inspected, completely belies its traditional appearance; it has the thickness of a two- or three-leaved brick wall but not its weight, for it is hollow with barely a two-inch membrane of concrete front and back. It is an extremely ingenious method of construction and shows that, behind traditional appearances, Ransome was still experimenting and developing. By now the internal construction was also in concrete, to judge from late work in the rusticated mode that I have seen, though still conceived as a system built up from separate concrete components rather than as a continuous and monolithic frame. Nevertheless, this continuation of traditional modes of thinking even in a non-traditional material only serves to further confuse the relationship of Ransome to the traditions of American industrial architecture up to his time.

The use of a pitched and clerestoried roof with visible end gables, for instance, was not uncommon, and anyone who knows the older industrial areas of the United States will know many such buildings. But they will not commonly be multi-story buildings, of the type that Ransome was building around the Bay Area; the pitched and clerestoried roof most frequently belongs to single-story worksheds, such as foundries and molding shops. In those older industrial areas back East, the multi-story mill or warehouse structure had, with very few exceptions, a flat-roofed profile or used an upstand parapet around the top of the walls to make its low roof pitches invisible from outside. Where there is a visible pitched roof, as on some of the older mills in Lowell, Massachusetts, it tends to be mansarded, giving a much flatter profile. The reasons for such profiles might possibly include a conscious aesthetic or stylistic preference, but there is a compelling economic reason as well: much of the floor space in the attic story would be too low for anyone to stand upright if the roof sloped down to an eavesplate level with the floor, and few industrialists would be willing to build that much wasteful volume.

It seems clear that the emergence of the flat-topped profile was a mostly American affair and came in with the general rationalization of factory and mill building procedures in the 1820s that, together with the use of a heavy timber internal frame for fireproofing reasons, can be lumped together as "regular mill construction." That term applies, technically, only to the timber internal frame, but it can stand here for a significantly American development in the construction of large industrial works.

Before that time, American industrial building was little differentiated from the general tradition of large-scale utilitarian constructions that runs back through the mill buildings of early industrialization in Britain and beyond that to the brick and stone warehouses of the Baltic and North Sea ports. Described in words, it is liable to sound like nothing more than the way people had to build anyhow; one could properly say that, in England, a Georgian house and a Georgian factory would, of necessity, be built in the same way. And not just in England; the first premises occupied in 1875 by the Larkin Company, on Chicago Street in Buffalo, illustrated in Sigfried Giedion's *Space, Time and Architecture*[4] and still standing during my time in that city, was built of brick and timber with segmented door and window openings, just like a regular eighteenth-century row house in Boston or even London.

Nevertheless, one can sense the emergence of a separate and parallel tradition, even in Europe, for the larger type of utilitarian structure well before the end of the eighteenth century; J. M. Richards's classic study *The Functional Tradition* (1958) abounds in examples that could never be mistaken for domestic structures even though the constructional procedures and all the architectural elements are identical. The evolution of the alternative tradition may well have its origins in dockside warehouses. The oldest I have seen are on the Nyhavn in Copenhagen, Denmark; the earliest were built before 1700. They are of brick, often with protective stone trim on the ground floors; their windows have regular segmented heads; the internal structures are of heavy timbers with, however, comparatively narrow bay widths of ten to twelve feet.

Their most notably "industrial" aspect, apart from their lack of ornamentation, is their height, which may be as much as six stories, under a tall and very visible tiled roof, which is their most obvious difference from their later American descendants. Their great height must have arisen largely from two obvious economic considerations: competitive pressure on expensive land at the water's edge and a relatively primitive technology for moving goods. The two things work together; what made waterside land so valuable was the comparative diseconomy of moving goods any distance horizontally on land; the traditional ratio that I was taught in grammar-school geography is that it was ten times more costly to move goods by land than by water, so there would be good reasons for locating the warehouse as close to the ship as possible.

In addition, moving goods vertically by cranes was a good deal more convenient, and capital intensive rather than labor intensive, than moving them horizontally in carts or on pack animals. This was certainly one of the main recommendations of this building format as a way of housing manufacturing industry. It also produced the most conspicuous variation from a perfectly regular system of identical fenestration from end to end of the building: the insertion of vertical stacks of larger openings to serve as hoisting doors through which goods could be swung in or out when hanging from the crane, which was usually a simple, swivelling, triangular bracket mounted above the highest door.

That kind of purely verbal description could apply almost equally well, two hundred years later, to structures such as housed the Buffalo Weaving and Belt Company plant of 1896. However, the physical structure of the version that appeared there alongside the Belt Line Railroad tracks, which made the suburbanization of Buffalo industries possible, had been transformed by vast refinements, subtle improvements, and, above all, rigorous rationalization. For, looking along the more than quarter-mile sequence of contiguous buildings occupied by Buffalo Weaving and built over a period of less than fifteen years, one could see exactly what rigorous rationalization could do to industrial building in an era of improved horizontal transporation. Ultimately, it would kill off the multi-story type with its cranes and hoisting doors (which survived vestigially on the tracks side of the oldest block) and replace it with the single-story workshed, where everything moved horizontally from truck dock to truck dock.

While such improved transportation was lacking, however, or until its potential was properly understood, the multi-story factory reigned supreme. It gave the world its standard imagery of the horrors of "Smoketown" with its "dark, satanic mills," but it also gave the standard images of prosperity: the panorama of row upon superimposed row of regular lighted windows, under the smoke belching merrily from hundreds of smokestacks ("merrily" because it meant all boilers were fired and everyone was working). Throughout northern England, Lowland Scotland, large tracts of northwestern Europe and almost the whole of the northeastern United States, the multi-story mill or factory flourished as one of the most successful (in terms of Darwinian survival) vernacular building types in the recent history of architecture. Local variations and detailing notwithstanding, the demand for rational construction and rationalized production processes, combined with the need for compact plans, meant that whether built of brick or stone, with an internal structure of wood or iron, its overall form would be pretty well invariant, wherever it stood upon the Earth's surface.

The compact type of plan, inherited, along with its multi-story height, from its warehouse origins, was of peculiar and increasing value to industry as mechanization and concentration increased. During the period of water mills as prime movers, the efficient use of the power from the mill wheel required that the works be built close to the mill race and dam. This could sometimes put as severe a pressure on difficult sites as had been the case with dockside building. Ideally the plant should be built right over the dam, and competition for such locations, in narrow and precipitous mill valleys, was so sharp that in parts of New England, for instance, usable mill sites became known as "privileges" and their use was formally legislated.

Two other considerations had greater consequence: distribution of power within the plant and the availability of light at the individual work station. While power from the mill wheel, or later the main steam engine, had to be distributed by shafting throughout the works and then taken off by belts and pulley wheels to individual machines, power losses through friction, etc., could best be reduced by keeping the number of shafts to a minimum, ideally one main power shaft per machine floor. This, inevitably, encouraged long buildings of comparatively thin section with the machines disposed along the power shafts, frequently in a double file on either side of them. The need for adequate lighting also encouraged fairly thin buildings, since this would put more of the work stations near an outer wall and thus, with luck, near a window.

Even when buildings were very large, as in the highly rationalized mills in Lowell, Massachusetts, they tended to be only four or five window bays thick. Such depths were of little more than domestic scale, as were the story-heights (twelve to fifteen feet); and the total heights of such structures—four to seven stories was the common range—were again little beyond the domestic range as exemplified in tenements or apartment blocks for urban locations. The workplace was not, in many ways, all that different from the buildings where the workers ate and slept and raised their families. Those who know Raymond Boulevard, along the river in Newark, New Jersey, will recall a sequence of three multi-story brick buildings, all remarkably similar in build and appearance: two of them are factories, but the other, number 627, is a well-made tenement for workers.

Buildings of this type, the "regular mills" of "regular mill construction," were the "former tradition" to which reference was made at the beginning of this chapter. Because they were a sound economic proposition, they existed long enough as individual structures—and as a type—to become a tradition. Available construction methods and materials had already been pushed almost to their limits when the basic type was stabilized in the 1820s, so it was unlikely to be disturbed by any major technical developments until new materials became available. Its long life was a tribute to its fundamental suitability and adaptability, but its limitations were far more severe than may be apparent to the modern visitor, who tends to encounter it only in its glamorized and romanticized afterlife, gussied up as a stylish boutiquerie, or with its ancient bricks scrubbed naked and its noble timbers educationally exposed in their last mortal incarnation as the Visitor Orientation Center of an Historic Industrial District.

The brightness of modern electric lighting effectively, paradoxically, and appropriately obscures what was clearly perceived as the main defect of the regular mill type in the days when less efficient forms of illumination were all that could be had: inadequate daylighting. Even before regular mill construction was finally replaced by concrete-framed structures, the search for wider windows forced modifications of the external walls of the regular mill that drove the structural performance of brick and masonry to their last limits. In the process, the wall underwent a kind of terminal transfiguration which, almost coincidentally, prefigures the concrete frame and is indeed imitated in some transitional examples of concrete construction.

In this final version, the solid wall pierced by windows (the kind of wall that Ransome had effectively imitated in concrete) was replaced by a system of separate brick columns, connected by thinner membranes of brickwork containing windows that went almost from pier to pier. In this way the weight of brickwork that had to be supported by the arch or beam that spanned each opening could be reduced to the minimum required for decent weatherproofing, but the stability of the wall as a whole was guaranteed by

Brick-pier-construction factory at Grosvenor and North Division, Buffalo, New York (destroyed by explosion, 1984). (Photo, Bazelon)

the thickness of the piers. And that guarantee was real—I have seen walls of this type in semi-ruinous structures leaning seven or eight degrees out of plumb and still holding together. The means of spanning over the windows and supporting the brickwork above were various: short concrete beams in some very late examples, steel or wrought-iron angles in some earlier examples. The old Iroquois Door and Lumber plant in Buffalo, reputedly designed by Louise Blanchard Bethune herself, was a model of puritanically stern, rectangular discipline, achieved by using concealed metal angles for the spans and plain stone sills under the windows. Not a curve was to be seen in its long brick facade, and it was strong enough to survive a major fire that took the top two floors off the plant in the early 1920s.

But it was a building catty-corner across the street from Iroquois Door that properly introduced me to the ingenuities of brick-pier construction, that showed me what strength resided in the tradition concrete was to replace and the ways in which that tradition was linked to the grand old traditions of architecture. That building, or buildings, had been part of the large manufacturing and shipping complex of the Larkin Company, an enterprise that tends to live in ill-conceived infamy in the minds of American lovers of architecture because "they had a Frank Lloyd Wright building and they had to go and pull it down!" The vicissitudes of that company, which in 1919 was the largest mail-order business in the history of Business, and the sad demise of its most famous structure, Wright's A Administration block of 1904–1906, constitute a saga that need not detain us here. What is of concern to this study is that the rest of the Larkin plant was almost intact, though mostly in constant peril, when I arrived in Buffalo, and it provided a kind of monumental history of American industrial architecture on either side of the changeover from regular mill construction to concrete.

The heart of this massive survival was a gigantic structure, some three-quarters of a million square feet in floor area, mostly of seven or eight stories, built in stages over a period of more than decade, and, by the end of the campaign in

Aerial view of Larkin plant, Buffalo, New York in 1924.

1907, occupying a complete city block along Seneca Street. The Larkin Company had labeled it with a letter code identifying its parts as separate buildings (a legal fiction for fire-insurance purposes), but the common voice of the Seneca Street community referred to it simply *en bloc* as 701 Seneca.

All save a small but instructive part of it (which will need comment later) was built in a coherent and consistent form of updated regular mill construction. Internally it was framed in steel: columns, beams, and secondary joists. Such construction is not fireproof in itself. Unlike the heavy timbers of wooden mill construction, which charred or burned slowly and often retained their structural strength long enough for the building to be emptied of goods and workers, naked steel construction would begin to twist, distort, and pull the building to pieces even before it melted. To obviate this it had to be clad in a fireproof and heat-retardant material. At 701 Seneca this was a coating of gypsum plaster that wrapped the metal so thickly that the columns, for instance, were the same fourteen-inch-square section as their wooden predecessors, while the primary beams that spanned between them and supported the secondaries and the built-up concrete and timber floors above were almost equally massive in appearance. The entire structure was immensely strong, capable of accepting a minimum floor load of 125 lb/ft^2 anywhere and over 300 in special areas. The whole enormous building gave an impression of imperturbable solidity that was confirmed by the fact that it was still in excellent condition after fifty years of very indifferent maintenance.

That impression derived overwhelmingly from the mode of construction of the exterior wall, insofar as it could be seen behind later stucco and alleged "modernizations" or on the adjoining buildings that were constructed in the same way. This was a brick-pier system, using quite massive piers of square section built out of high-grade engineering brick of a dark brown hue. All exposed arrises were rounded off with "bull-nosed" stock, leaving no unguarded corners to be spalled off by the frosts and rigors of Buffalo's notoriously severe winters.

Larkin L and M warehouse block,
Buffalo, New York, by R. J. Reidpath
and Son, 1902–4. (Photo, Bazelon)

Larkin *L* and *M* block, pilaster wall construction. (Photo, Bazelon)

Between the piers the thickness of the wall was reduced by one brick front and back to produce the segmental arch that spanned the window opening and the spandrel wall that protected the edge of the floor slab above and carried the sill of the next tier of windows. Under this wide segmental arch, and strengthening it, no doubt, were two subsidiary arches carried on a common central column that divided the window into halves. This part was also reduced in thickness by one brick back and front, so that the central mullion was a square, two bricks wide, again with bull-nosed corners since this was standard for outside corners throughout the work.

This subtle and carefully modulated system—which gives maximum thickness and strength at the piers but minimum "tunnelling" of the light at the windows, where the brickwork is only four bricks thick—seems to be a distillation of the accumulated wisdom of some three centuries of brick building, but with the radical addition of the ability or willingness to apply critical intelligence to time-honored usages if their performance could thereby be improved. Demanding comparison with Roman construction in its last radical phases under Diocletian, this too seems to represent a long-sustained vernacular at its most refined.

One must recognize, however, that the refinement was as conscious here as it must have been in Rome; the work of professionals, it reminds us that *vernacular* is a word to be applied only with great wariness to American industrial work of this period. Since there is so much building of this type, if rarely this quality, to be seen all over the old industrial Northeast, and since it so often appears to be merely common practice rather than inspired design, it is easy to suppose it must all have been done by custom and precedent by honest craftsmen and hard-nosed entrepreneurs, without professional help. Yet the bulk of it was designed by professional engineers and architects. In the case of 701 Seneca, it was the remarkably resourceful local architects R. J. Reidpath and Son (who, in one of their other roles, were the structural engineers for the famous house that Frank Lloyd Wright designed for Darwin Martin, Larkin's managing director). As designers for industry, the Reidpaths showed a telling mixture of conservatism and adventure—reluctant to abandon tried and economical traditional usages, but not loath to investigate new and reasonable ones that promised assured profit for their clients and themselves.

Parenthetically, this tendency to retain useful traditional usages even in innovative circumstances is best seen in the Reidpath attitude to rusticated stonework. Before 1900 they were prepared to design whole factories in solid rusticated masonry. The one I knew best until it was demolished in 1983 was Buffalo Veneer Company, next to the Belt Line Railroad on Main Street: a three-story facade twenty-five window bays long, its absolute rectangularity broken only by a pediment of sorts over the central three windows. The walls were of regularly coursed rough-faced stones, with single slabs serving as sills and window heads. The work may have lacked the grandeur of Boston's celebrated granite masonry—the local stone used in Buffalo is gritty and ungracious—but it was all well laid and done with high professionalism.

The schooling in stonework on which these skills depended was, in fact, a standard Buffalo and western New York usage of purely utilitarian intention without apparent aesthetic overtones—the use of stone foundation walls in brick factories. Nearly all such structures in Buffalo have their brickwork founded on some four feet of the gritty local capstone, laid in regular courses about eight inches deep. Only about half this depth of stonework is below ground; the upper part is exposed, usually up to the level of the first internal floor. The 701 Seneca building has such foundation coursing visible all round, as does Iroquois Door and Lumber. The latter demonstrates another functional reason for leaving the upper few courses exposed: Iroquois Door is scrupulously detailed to prevent damage to the brickwork by the wheels and (in those days) iron tires of carts and trucks. It has angle irons to protect the edges of door openings and neat cast-iron "spats" protecting the bottoms of columns between loading docks. The rest of its perimeter is defended

Iroquois Door and Lumber Company, Buffalo, New York, by Bethune, Bethune, and Fuchs, 1898? (Photo, Bazelon)

Iroquois Door and Lumber Company, doorway and construction detail. (Photo, Bazelon)

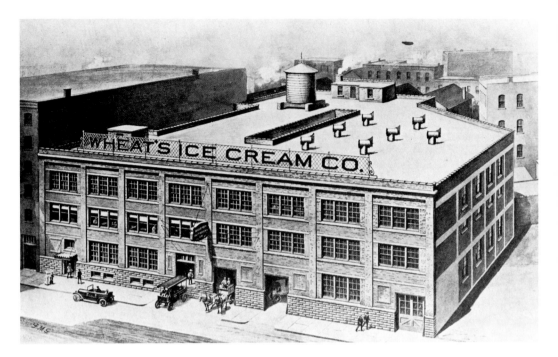

Wheat's Ice Cream Company, first block, Buffalo, New York, by R. J. Reidpath and Son, 1911. (From *The Industrial Empire of Niagara*, 1919)

by the projecting three or four courses of foundation-wall stonework, a much tougher and wear-resistant material than even good quality brick.

When the Reidpath office, in step with the rest of the profession, changed over to concrete framing around 1910, they continued to add aprons of stonework around the bases of their buildings, even when there was little brickwork visible on the increasingly wide-windowed walls above. This may have been pure stylistic conservatism, and would probably have been decried as just that by modernist critics of the twenties and thirties, but in the context of the continuing tradition of industrial construction, it can equally well be seen as the retention of a functionally useful device to protect the client's investment in the building against unnecessary wear and tear.

This *ad hoc* mixture of the respectably ancient (rusticated masonry) and the still daringly modern (the concrete frame) is noteworthy because it is one of the more accessible indicators of the attitudes with which American industrial builders may have entered the epoch in which they were to have a worldwide influence on modern architecture. European modernists, looking across the full width of the Atlantic and in almost complete ignorance of the former tradition, might have believed that what they saw was radical, unprecedented, and revolutionary; but on its territory and in context, it looks no more radical, no more innovative, than was needed to ensure, step by step, competitive economies for the clients. Hard-nosed patrons and the architects who served them conserved traditional usages that were still serviceable. They had no ideological axes to grind, no revolutionary postures to maintain, even if they knew—as Ransome did at the end of his life—that revolutions in industrial architecture had been wrought. Piecemeal, the dynamics of building in a market economy at a time of rapid technological advance would produce every aspect of an architectural revolution except the revolutionary intent. The rationality of the economic/industrial system that these architects served, required of them—as a daily commonplace—innovations as constant as any European futurist of the day could demand as prerequisites for some distant but desired utopia.

One should also recall that these architects functioned in cities that might be growing, prosperous, and progressive, but were also remarkably provincial and remote from metropolitan centers of cultural and political thought. Where they held fast to traditional forms and usages, to cornices and segmental arches and rustication, it was not likely to be solely or absolutely for the sake of economy. It was the architecture in which these men had been trained, the only architecture they knew in many cases; and among an insecure, philistine, or *nouveau riche* local society, skill in handling them could reassure architects and clients alike of cultural roots and professional expertise. Certainly the architects enjoyed the freedoms of their isolation; they were spared the jealousies and peer-pressures of their metropolitan contemporaries and could eventually come to enjoy positions closer to the real wielders of effective economic and political power in smaller cities where "everybody knew everybody." But as the case of Albert Kahn in Detroit shows, being close to powerful and innovative magnates like Henry Ford did nothing to break up the stylistic timidity he showed in all buildings that were not hidden from the public eye. Few of the architects who ultimately *produced* the revolution in industrial architecture seem ever to have *demanded* a revolution in the manner of Frank Lloyd Wright or some of his European contemporaries.

On the other hand, it is not always easy to demonstrate that the retention of trusted usages and forms derived from an explicit desire for reassurance. As the Reidpaths' rustication shows, these usages were so much part and parcel of the former tradition that they do constitute something like a vernacular, in spite of their professional origins, and one hesitates to isolate them as purely aesthetic features or architectural symbols. Yet on the occasions where one may be excused from this hesitation, it is usually because what is going on is abundantly clear. A resounding example is the great Pillsbury A mill in Minneapolis, designed before 1885 by the ever-marginal and provincial Leroy S. Buffington. Sited on the cliff on the Minneapolis side of the river above the falls, it was a gesture of defiance against the Washburn Mills on the opposite bank. Designed to be seen from the St. Paul side, it presents its "best facade," of good gray stone, toward the river. The conventionally regular fenestration of that public elevation is dramatically broken by an unabashedly architectural gesture—not daring or innovative, but one of learned traditionalism: a four-light, semicircular Roman "thermal" window. It looks very good, entirely at home and appropriate among the more modest features of the rest of the facade. And, accidentally, it reminds us that these structures have roots in history, not only by virtue of the continuous, quasi-vernacular constructional tradition to which they belong, but also by way of the academic traditions their designers would inevitably have encountered in their training, whether in academe or through pupilage in an architect's office.

There is yet another connection that may be at work here: within academe itself, rationalism and neoclassicism are never far apart. Products of the same epoch of European architectural development in the Age of Reason, they have

Pillsbury A Mill, Minneapolis, Minnesota, by Leroy S. Buffington, 1881 or later. (Photo, Bazelon)

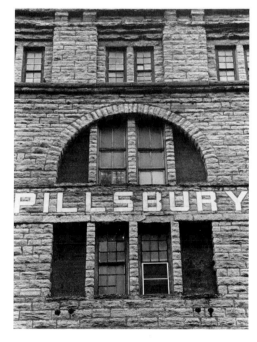

Pillsbury A Mill, the Roman window. (Photo, Bazelon)

constantly rediscovered one another ever since. So when rational, late-Victorian industry sought to lend itself architectural dignity and decorum, it did not necessarily have to do so by adding a profusion of ornament (which might have alarmed cost-conscious clients): it could look within the double traditions of rationalism and neoclassicism, constructional vernacular and conventional learning, and rediscover—as Piranesi and Sir John Soane had done so much earlier—the authority of Roman construction, naked and unadorned.

If one sought a properly prestigious Roman monument that would be relevant to these industrial aspirations, it would surely be the fourth-century Basilica at Trier, whose side walls are a perfect prototype for brick-pier construction. Whether any American factory builder of the nineteenth century was actually acquainted with the Basilica at first hand is doubtful, though not impossible, but illustrations of it could certainly be found in many libraries in architecture schools and academies of art. At some half-forgotten level, such knowledge of the historical past was probably always available to reinforce the hands and minds of factory architects when they needed it. Leroy Buffington's grand but austere Roman window may have quite a history behind it, and so may many other practices of the tradition on which the work of innovators like Ransome was to be founded.

Clean, Well-lighted Places

However secure the former tradition, with its habits of adaptive pragmatism and its inherited vocabulary of architectural forms, may have appeared at the very beginning of the present century, it was to be overthrown by a genuine revolution in material and concepts between 1902 and 1906. The nature of that revolution and the profundity of its consequences are epitomized within the vast bulk of 701 Seneca. A couple of years after the completion of the main building campaign in 1907, the company cleared the site of the last remnant of the previous generation of buildings, the old boiler house, which had been replaced by a new and large power house immediately to the west of 701. The cleared site was little more than a notch in the back wall of the monster, seven stories high but less than fifty feet wide, and the company filled it with the new Building C to render the work floors continuous across what had been a profitless interruption.

Against the grain of all the previous brick-pier construction by the Reidpaths on the 701 Seneca site, the company's own design staff, and their contractors, devised three bays of concrete-framed construction of absolute simplicity. The openings to the outside were glazed clear across from column to column and from the underside of the floor slab above down to a sill that topped a low brick spandrel wall just high enough to carry a hot water radiator. The environmental transformation wrought by this innovation could be seen at 701 Seneca as nowhere else in the world, because the fully glazed concrete insert of Building C was entirely surrounded by works in the former tradition—with windows tunnelled through a massive brick wall—and one could walk through directly from the old into the new or vice

Larkin C Building, Buffalo, New York, 1913, present state. (Photo, Bazelon)

Larkin N Building, Buffalo, New York; interior showing daylighting through brick exterior wall. (Photo, author)

Larkin C Building; interior showing level of daylighting using reinforced concrete frame. Photograph taken at the same aperture and shutter speed as the picture above and under identical external lighting conditions.

versa. The difference in daylighting levels could only be described as sensational. Whereas natural light of usable
strength barely penetrated the depth of one fourteen-foot
bay from the twinned windows of the brick-pier section, it
penetrated better than twice that depth from the wall-to-
wall and ceiling-high glazing in Building C, and with far less
glare because there were no immediate contrasts of jux-
taposed light and dark to distress the eyes. Unfortunately,
this invaluable historical demonstration can no longer be observed: conventional postmodern wisdom about energy con-
servation caused these wide areas of glazing to be bricked
up almost completely in the early 1980s, leaving window
openings even smaller than those of the rest of the block.
But while the glass walls remained unobscured, one could
certainly see what made the Daylight factory, for all its high
heat losses in the cold of winter, such a compellingly attractive proposition to entrepreneurs and the work force alike.

By 1911, the year in which the Larkin Company decided
to make their last section of 701 Seneca out of concrete,
the virtues of the Daylight factory were just beginning to appear as received wisdom in professional and trade magazines:

*Pure, clear, uncolored daylight—the sunshine of roofless fields
which doubtless contributes in no small measure to the rare ar-
tisanship of Japanese, Indian and Italian handiwork—is becoming the possession of the American factory laborer. Steel sash
windows which are weatherproof, give access to a maximum of
daylighting*

wrote *The American Architect and Building News* in a mildly
poetic vein not unknown in its editorials of the period. It
went on to assert that

*If the books were to be examined and an accountant rendered a
verdict, the issue might not be entirely clear or decisive, but if
the votes of the people connected with the factory were taken
there would be no question . . . but that whatever additional
expenditure may have been required was fully justified in the
improved health, the improved moral, physical and aesthetic
conditions.*[5]

Though the revolution in industrial building went well beyond daylighting as such, in many eyes that was clearly the outstanding innovation. To provide daylighting of the kind and volume that was now expected, a steel-framed building would need a steel-framed exterior as well, and that, for fireproofing as well as less tangible reasons, seemed to be virtually inconceivable in the first decade of the twentieth century. Yet it had been done here and there: as early as 1898 the old Veeder cyclometer plant at Hartford, Connecticut, had a pure steel frame lightly clad in brick. Furthermore, "in the design of the building, one of the principal ideas was that it should have an abundance of light on every square foot of floor space, so that it could all be available for carrying out the very fine operations required for the manufacture of cyclometers."[6]

This must have been one of the earliest successful attempts to build a true Daylight factory, one in which every square inch of the exterior envelope that could reasonably be glazed was filled with glass. That *Engineering News* found it worthy of commentary and illustration (no doubt prompted by the enterprising Berlin Bridge Co., who built the frame) may indicate that it was the first of its type. Its subsequent disappearance from the literature, modernist or otherwise, seems equally noteworthy. If the early creation of steel and glass structures almost of itself guarantees builders a place in the canon of pioneers of the modern movement, why has Veeder been forgotten while the somewhat later Fischer Marble Company plant in the Bronx still tends to receive at least a footnote mention.[7] The answer may be that in the Fischer plant, the steel was clearly exposed on the exterior of the building, whereas at Veeder it was, not unreasonably, skinned with one leaf of brick.

For that reason, Fischer answered the modernist demand for "honesty of structural expression" while Veeder did not. One must note that this demand has never affected the reputation of, say, Louis Sullivan as a pioneer of modern design; indeed, he is conventionally praised for honesty in spite of the fact that the supporting steel of his buildings is never seen, is obfuscated in his elevations by the use of alternate dummy piers that do not carry weight, and applies only to the visible facades of his buildings, as nothing but the cheapest form of enclosure is used on the rear elevations. A more valid point in Fischer's favor, however, was that its structural system was ingenious and elegant, whereas the only illustration I have seen of the Veeder building shows it to have been a comparatively dull design. And one point that must be carried against them both is that only under special circumstances could a completely steel-framed building be considered adequately fireproof.

That Veeder was favorably received when built but ignored by the modernists may also be due to another interesting aspect of the tradition immediately preceding the concrete revolution—its extraordinary eclecticism in the use of materials. Whatever the obvious gains of building the whole structure out of a single material, to do so was visibly against what had become customary operating procedures by the end of the century. Admixture of different materials, each well adapted to its particular structural function and location, was normal and was often admirable in its sophistication and unshackled inventiveness. It was also, of course, another aspect of the tradition's conservative preference for proven solutions.

The most exemplary case of such constructional eclecticism known to me personally is the old Keystone plant on Chandler Street in Buffalo, which still stands, though much altered now. It was a single-story clerestory production shed—the format of the future, as it was to turn out—built just after the turn of the century. Its external walls were of entirely traditional brick construction, complete with stone basement courses, buttresses, corbelling, and segmentally arched windows. The nearly flat outer slopes of the roof were supported on four-inch square hollow cast-iron columns such as I have not seen elsewhere, carrying conventional steel I-beams on which the roof decking was laid. The clerestory itself, instead of being of continuously framed glazing consistent with any of the structure below, was a brick-walled structure, standing on two I-beams that run the length of the building, with separate windows set into the brickwork! Since this clerestory structure was entirely without inherent lateral stiffness, and could have been blown down by a moderate gale, it was diagonally braced at intervals with crossed tie-rods, complete with turnbuckles to adjust their lengths and tensions—perhaps the most enterprising invention in the whole performance.

For concrete construction to prevail against such sophisticated and well-founded ingenuity, it had to offer some striking advantages. At first sight the most paradoxical, yet ultimately the most fundamental, was that it rendered most such ingenuities unnecessary and therefore, economically speaking, obsolete. To build in a single material with a single technique would entail less complex specification writing, costing, and site supervision and require far fewer skilled trades, and should thus prove simpler and therefore faster and therefore cheaper. It did finally prove to have all these qualities, but only after the industry had become more familiar with it. The number of spectacular collapses, some of them repeat performances on the same site, reported in trade and professional magazines of the period force one to conclude that the Age of the Pioneers around 1900 must also have been the Age of Faith!

Speed and economy were put first in the fairly impressive roster of improvements that were supposed to accompany the change to concrete-framed construction, in the view of the editors of *The American Architect and Building News*. They listed the advantages of the new material as "first, speedy erection; second, low first cost; third, daylight illumination; fourth, [earthquake] shock-proofness; fifth, maintenance economy; and, sixth, fireproofness."[8] For preventing earthquake damage, concrete offered few decisive advantages over properly designed steelwork, to judge from what survived, say, the massive shocks of the San Francisco earthquake of 1906. A case could still be made for steel construction in Daylight factories, as the Veeder plant shows. And the question of maintenance remains somewhat moot, given the short first-user life that most industrial construction in the United States in the twentieth century has usually enjoyed. Nearly all such buildings have normally been neglected from the time their original owners decided to dump them on the market, and the results reveal all too clearly that in most industrial environments, exposed concrete needs far more upkeep and protection against destructive atmospheres than its early champions were usually prepared to admit.

This, then, really leaves only fireproofing as the critical consideration in determining if the desired Daylight factory would be built of concrete. Experience showed that metallic construction usually had a far worse fire performance than the heavy timbers of regular mill construction. Timber deserved its epithet of slow-burning construction and retained its structural integrity for much of the time it was slowly burning, whereas noncombustible metals proved to be dangerous under conditions of great heat: cast iron would shatter, wrought iron and steel would distort and deform. Of course steel could be fireproofed, otherwise regular skyscraper construction would have been far too dangerous to be acceptable or—what was more vital—to be insurable. But the cost of fireproofing skyscraper construction was largely concealed by the fact that social and architectural custom required such structures to be clad in ornamentation without and have tolerable surfaces within. It was only when Mies van der Rohe wished to exhibit the steel frames of his Chicago towers in the 1950s that the fireproofing of skyscrapers became an issue rather than a by-product of customary practice.

In the industrial buildings of the former tradition, such amenities were minimal on the exteriors and nonexistent for interiors, so the cost of wrapping structural steel in gypsum plaster inside, and brick, terra-cotta, tiling, or patent cement outside, was a visible budget item that might be tolerated for public facades or street fronts but nowhere else on the structure. The concrete frame avoided the expense of such added protection by being inherently fireproof, and probably ingratiated itself with many industrial builders for another and apparently unconnected reason: the dimensions for a reasonably strong, economical, and fireproof concrete upright usually came somewhere near to the fourteen-inch-square dimension that everybody already knew well from slow-burning timber construction and from fireproofed steel-work. When all these considerations of speed, economy, daylighting, maintenance, seismic stability, and so forth are added to fireproofing, there was a small advantage for reinforced concrete construction in industrial building, an advantage that would probably have grown at some cautious pace in step with industry's growing familiarity with the material and confidence in its reliability but for a dramatic event that seems to have changed opinions coast to coast.

In 1902 the East Coast plant of Pacific Coast Borax, at Bayonne, New Jersey, went up in a spectacular fire that attracted national attention because it was so hot that steel twisted and iron melted into shapeless puddles on the floor. But the floors survived and so did the internal columns and external walls because they were all made of the same material, fireproof reinforced concrete. There could have been no more convincing demonstration of the virtues of the material, but over and above the incontrovertible (and photographable) physical fact of the building's almost complete survival, the concrete industry took full advantage of this free gift of favorable publicity. The Atlas Portland Cement Company saw to it that this would be the best-known conflagration of the new century and gave it a full chapter in their 1907 publication *Reinforced Concrete in Factory Construction.* At the back of the volume is a lengthy testimonial letter, which deserves extensive quotation. After conventional salutations appropriate to a solicited testimonial, the manager of the eastern division of Pacific Coast Borax writes:

Among some of the special features that occur to us are:

First: Its being absolutely fireproof. This was fully tested as you well know by the fire which we had in our Calcining Department . . . a fire of terrific heat—melting all exposed metal and burning all combustible partitions etc., that the building at that time contained; but the concrete building itself stood the test magnificently, and as our property is surrounded by stills of the Standard Oil Co., this is particularly important to us, and we know that our building is absolutely fireproof.

Second: Cost of repairs. No expenditure under this heading is made—the building being monolithic and like Spanish Wine, improves with age.

Third: Strength. As you know we carry terrific loads on our floors —on our fourth floor carrying a weight of 1430 lbs. per sq. ft. On the lower floors we have carried much heavier weights without straining the building in the least.

Fourth: Cleanliness. Your construction is an ideal construction for a factory as it can be kept perfectly clean—it being a simple matter to hose and wash it out.

We believe that concrete construction is the proper construction and that the Ransome system is the best system.[9]

Not surprisingly, this testimonial had originally been solicited by the Ransome and Smith Company, by then established in New York.

The Pacific Coast Borax fire was, it appears, the triumph and vindication of Ransome's professional life. That company's building at Bayonne, erected in 1897, had been his first work on the East Coast and is also reputedly the first complete reinforced concrete factory to be erected on that side of the country. The fire and Ransome's great and growing reputation as an inventor and constructor combined to give a kind of charisma to reinforced concrete as the material of the new industrial age; and Ransome was only one of a number of forceful new engineering personalities who appeared upon the scene as exponents and exploiters of this seemingly miraculous material. The outstanding American theorist of the time was undoubtedly L. G. Heidenreich of Chicago, who also controlled the licensing in the United States of the Monier patents for cylindrical constructions. Among practitioners, Ransome's sometime-disciple C. A. P. Turner of Minneapolis, American pioneer of the mushroom column and flat slab floor, and the brothers Albert and Julius Kahn of Detroit, architect and proprietor of the Trussed Concrete system patents respectively, were the most innovative of the younger industrial builders in concrete.

Ransome, however, was the *doyen* of the profession, resplendent in the glory of the fire and his huge roster of patents. More to the point, he was also poised on the edge of

Ernest L. Ransome's trade plate,
1906. (Photo, author)

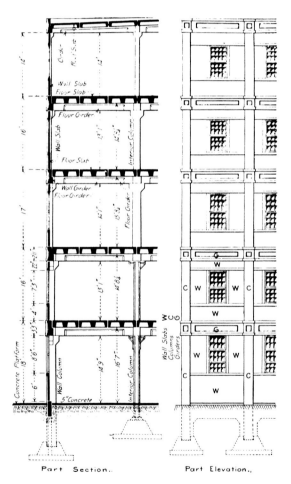

Part Section.   Part Elevation.,

"Unit Construction System," 1906.
(From *Reinforced Concrete Buildings*,
1912)

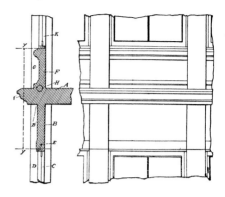

Patented system for projecting floor
slabs, Ernest L. Ransome. 1902.
(From *Reinforced Concrete Buildings*,
1912)

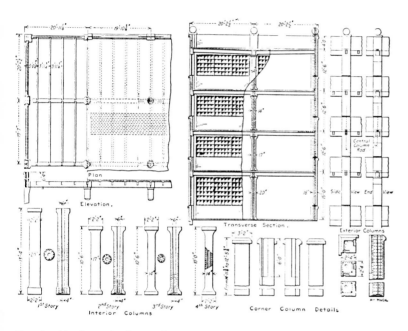

Complete kit of parts for Ransome's
Patent System, 1903. (From *Reinforced Concrete Buildings*, 1912)

the most extraordinarily creative part of his career in the actual design of buildings, the years between 1903 and 1906, in which he delivered the fireproof, daylit, concrete-framed factory in what was to prove to be its canonical form. Fortunately the two crucial buildings of the period still survive at the time of this writing. One is the second phase of Pacific Coast Borax at Bayonne, undertaken immediately after the fire; and the other is the enormous plant in Beverly, Massachusetts, for the United Shoe Machinery Company—the firm that in 1910 would put up most of the financing for Gropius's Faguswerk, the design that stands, debatably, at the beginning of the "Americanization" of European modern architecture.

The United Shoe Machinery plant, begun in 1903 and complete enough to be used by the company in 1906 (extensions in the same style and construction system were to continue for decades) is a work whose appearance of crushing self-assurance belies some mystifications and inadequacies in the design, though none so grave as to perturb the admiration of all who know the work. Its absence from the general literature on the history of modern architecture is a permanent reproach to scholarship, for even on the score of stylistic "modernity," let alone technical proficiency and inventiveness, it is the match for anything built anywhere in the world at that time. Stylistically it is the most sophisticated of all his buildings, and even if the detailing is the work of bright younger assistants in the Ransome and Smith office, the result is still all of a piece with the design approach of the rest of his works.

The plant's three immensely long production blocks have three stories of "totally glazed" work space standing on a more solidly walled *basamento* pierced by Ransome's customary segmentally arched windows. Restrained string courses separate the fenestration of the main work floors from the *basamento* and from the frieze and drastically simplified coved cornice above. It is a stripped classicism visibly more self-assured than that of Auguste Perret, the honored *patron* of French concrete architecture in the same period, and, to me, entirely admirable in its appropriate mix-

United Shoe Machinery Company,
Beverly, Massachusetts, by Ernest L.
Ransome, 1903–6. (Photo, author)

United Shoe Machinery, detail of
facade. (Photo, author)

ture of decorum and puritanism. There are no architectural details, in any conventional sense, other than those listed above, and, like the plain square columns and the thinner mullions that occur at the half-bays, they are all crisply and unfussily delivered in excellent fair-face concrete work.

Between the three production blocks are linking blocks that break up the long intervening alleys to form courtyards or light wells (now glazed over), and here the detailing is somewhat different in style, if not in quality. On the front of one of the cross-blocks a small "front office" has been inserted in a slightly more elaborately detailed version of the general idiom. More telling is the detailing on the cross-blocks themselves, in a flat, pretty, pilastered Doric, simplified but unmistakable, with capitals and all; now battered and beaten up after eighty years of heavy industrial use, it wears a rather attractively Pompeian air of elegant and antique decay.

Such remnants of the former tradition are echoed in the internal work, though in an expectably plainer manner. The earlier parts have pre-cast beams dropped into the slotted heads of the columns, which are octagonal in section, and then grouted down to lock together the ends of the reinforcing rods. This built-up system is still only a transitional step toward the fully rationalized monolithic frames that were to appear soon after; vertical elements are not yet all the same in section, even internally, since columns that flank the wider circulation bays are circular in section, not octagonal. Just how transitional the whole design must be is indicated by the fact that the earliest building-permit drawings show substantially the same design—but in brick![10] The decision to build in concrete apparently came only after the Atlas Portland Cement Company made the firm an offer they couldn't refuse and brought Ransome in as the engineer, thus enabling all three parties to stage a formal demonstration of their prowess and set before the world a large and impressive structure that fully confirmed the promise of Pacific Coast Borax.

United Shoe Machinery, "Doric" details. (Photo, author)

United Shoe Machinery, service block at rear, before 1911. (Photo, author)

Impressive it undoubtedly is; sheer quality of construction and design, and the grandeur of its original conception put it in a different class from anything else done up to that time (Europeans should remember that in 1906 Peter Behrens had not yet built any of his supposedly epoch-making erection halls for the AEG heavy-product operations). But if one seeks the building that truly shows the workings of Ransome's mind when he finally achieves the Daylight factory, then one must look at the second phase of Pacific Coast Borax at Bayonne. Ransome's own comments on it, in *Reinforced Concrete Buildings*, show that he understood precisely what he had achieved:

The Pacific Coast Borax Co.'s building, at Bayonne, N.J., erected in 1897–1898, in a measure marks the closing of the old-time construction of concrete buildings, constructed more or less in imitation of brick or stone buildings, with comparatively small windows set in walls.[11]

In the caption to a picture on the facing page, he states the change even more clearly: "In Front, the original building of the old type. In Rear, a more recent addition of the modern type."

In the picture one can see that the old block is indeed of the type that Ransome had been building in the Bay Area. Even though it is not a clerestoried shed with gabled ends, its windows are narrow and have segmental heads (though arranged in triplets instead of regularly spaced in bays of even width), and its hollow walls are horizontally grooved to simulate rustication. Today only the back wall of this construction is still standing—the concrete work that resisted the "fire of terrific heat" fell to the wreckers during a reorganization of the plant layout in the 1960s. The surviving wall now serves simply as a closure to the otherwise open end of the "addition of the modern type." Yet this disregarded fragment has the enormous value of being the only known survivor of Ransome's "old-time construction." What was the outer, "rusticated" face of the wall, having been turned by the second phase into an interior face protected from weathering for more than eighty years, is still in good enough condition for the quality of the work to be ap-

Pacific Coast Borax Company, Bayonne, New Jersey, first phase, by
Ernest L. Ransome, 1897. (From
*Reinforced Concrete in Factory Con-
struction,* 1907)

Pacific Coast Borax, Bayonne, second phase, by Ernest L. Ransome,
1903. (From *Reinforced Concrete in
Factory Construction,* 1907)

The Daylight Factory   **73**

preciated. The imprint of the shuttering can also be seen, and—where it has been broken through during later alterations, for instance—the wall's hollow interior can still be inspected.

The second block, built in 1903, stands upon a basement in the same mode as the first and built as part of the original building campaign, apparently to await further developments—of which the fire was clearly the least expected. The upper three stories and attic of the second phase, quite apart from offering, for the first time, the external aspects of the true Daylight factory, have the historically unique interest of being the place where one can conveniently study Ransome's celebrated "patent system" in its purest surviving form. That system received the patents on its last remaining special components in 1903, the year the Bayonne II and Beverly plants were begun. Although Beverly publicly claimed to be in the system, and did indeed employ many of its larger pre-cast standardized components (wall panels, stairs), architectural and commercial ambition overran systemic purity and much of the work is not of standardized units but is special unto itself.

The far less ambitious Borax plant, isolated on its remote marshy site at the Bayonne "hook" and still neighbored by the installations of the Standard Oil Company, is very nearly the pure system and can be appreciated both as a constructional procedure and as an intellectual construct. As expounded in the text and illustrations of *Reinforced Concrete Buildings,*[12] as well as in the sequence of patent applications through 1902, the system was essentially a kit of parts—columns, etc.—to support a series of superimposed floors. Since the floors may project beyond the columns at the perimeter of the structure, the system resembles the Dom-ino system in which Le Corbusier was to be involved a decade later. But whereas the compelling power of the famous Dom-ino diagram lies precisely in its being so diagrammatic, a pure intellectual concept uncontaminated by details of practicality, the Ransome system bears all the marks of experience and consideration for what will happen on the building site. It offers, for instance, a number of different column types and column heights, all pre-cast, and mostly of a hollow, octagonal section apparently borrowed from the only body of pre-casting practice familiar to Ransome's generation of builders—cast iron, in which hollow formats had always been the normal practice.

It differs again in its floor-construction procedures. While United Shoe Machinery virtually reproduces the framing of regular mill construction in reinforced concrete and Dom-ino has flat slab floors, some of the patent drawings for the system show very deep beams of thin section placed almost as close together as the joists of a wooden deck in the former tradition. And there seems to be nothing in the system that requires the columns to be monolithic with the floors above and below. Inside Bayonne II all this can be seen in detail since most of the floors have been cleared out completely. The columns are indeed octagonal, with square bases and square "capitals" made of four straight sections of regular cyma-section moldings. The beams of the ceiling are almost two feet deep, barely four inches thick, spaced at less than two-foot intervals. They span transversely between similarly dimensioned longitudinal primary beams that are twinned, two to each row of column heads. Since these beams stand on the very edges of the square capitals, the section through which reinforcing rods could have been cast into the, as it were, box frame above during the pouring of the concrete is slender indeed, as are the reinforcing rods themselves. Where they can be seen, they prove to be not only of Ransome's unmistakable twisted square section (the subject of one of his earliest patents), but also remarkably thin, some apparently under a quarter inch in section.

Even if the floor section, with its neatly filleted internal corners, can be described as something like a box frame, the larger system one sees inside the building manifestly does not yet add up to a concrete frame in the standard modern understanding of that concept. It cannot be seen as a regular, rectangular, monolithic, three-dimensional grid of visually similar horizontals and verticals, containing or defining an equally regular and rectangular isotropic space. Ransome is simply stacking floor on column, column on floor, and the

Pacific Coast Borax, second phase,
present condition. (Photo, author)

Pacific Coast Borax, fire damage to
steel-framed equipment, 1902.
(From *Reinforced Concrete in Factory
Construction,* 1907)

effect is extraordinarily archaic—the long rows of classicizing columns on the empty upper floors recalling nothing so much as the interiors of great Roman granaries or cisterns, like the *Piscina Meravigliosa* at Baiae, outside Naples. Once again the old double tradition of rationalism/neoclassicism seems to reassert itself.

The specifically nineteenth-century tradition of the difference between the construction of the internal frame and the building of the exterior wall undergoes its final convulsion at Bayonne II, because the exterior wall as a separate architectural entity was to disappear in the pure application of the system. The most crucial aspect of the system in Ransome's mind was the floor slab, which in the patents he proposes to extend beyond the outer row of columns. The wall as a continuous structural entity is to be replaced by upstands and downstands in the plane of the outer columns and cast integrally with the floor slabs, with glazing spanning from column to column and from upstand below to downstand above. The projecting floor slabs were, inevitably, to be profiled with classical moldings, and the exterior of the structure would thus have emphasized the disappearance of the load-bearing wall and the new dominance of the floor slab.

This is not what one sees at Bayonne II; one sees something far more radical, caused by the simplification of what happens at the edge of the floor slab. First, the upstand and downstand have been eliminated; the space between floors is occupied by a pre-cast concrete panel with a wooden industrial sash above, both of which are carried in vertical slots cast into the sides of the columns. That looks like a practical refinement he must have chosen at a fairly early stage in the design, but it produced, conceptually, the all-glass, frame-and-fill wall so admired by modernists for its radicalism. Second, however, practical or economic consideration led to the elimination of the profiling on the projecting edges of the floor slabs; in fact, apart from a notional string course at the top of the basement left over from phase one and another at the level of the attic floor, the edges of the slabs are finished off flush with the outer faces of the external columns. Since these columns are square and present a flat sur-

Pacific Coast Borax, surviving hollow concrete wall of first phase. (Photo, author)

Pacific Coast Borax, interior of second phase. (Photo, author)

Pacific Coast Borax, floor-beam system in second phase. (Photo, author)

Pacific Coast Borax, capital of column in second phase. (Photo, author)

face to the exterior, as do the unprofiled edges of the floor slabs, what one sees on the outside of Bayonne II is a flat grid of apparently equal horizontals and verticals, the canonical image of the concrete frame. Externally, the block looks a decade more modern than it does inside, and its critically intermediate position is to be inferred by comparing interior and exterior. Its intermediate position is most of its significance to the historian, whatever its other virtues as a building. It stands at the exact point of the invention of the true concrete frame; it is unlike anything of Ransome's that came before, and it is not much like anything that anybody did later.

The one exception I know to that observation is another fascinatingly intermediate building, the Minterburn (or Roosevelt) Mills in Rockville, Connecticut. Built in 1906 by the contracting firm of Frank B. Gilbreth and designed by C. R. Makepeace and Co., engineers, the mill gains greatly by its site and context. Rockville is a classic river-valley mill town, though on a modest scale. It has twelve privileges, and the Minterburn Mill stands on the last and highest of them, appropriately closing a sequence that shows the whole history of New England mill building from the woodframed, clapboarded neo-Grec of the Hockanum and Saxony Mills of the 1830s and onward, through all the subsequent variations of style and materials. Minterburn is a very big structure for this part of the world: almost three hundred feet long and nearly sixty feet deep, it is five stories high at the upper end and six where it drops toward the mill race at the privilege.

At first sight it might be mistaken for a brick-pier structure that has been stuccoed and painted over, but beneath its smooth surface is well-finished concrete that has survived eighty years in excellent condition. The resemblance to a brick-pier construction is caused by the fenestration, which instead of being broad and "modern" is tall and narrow as in the carrying-wall structures of the former tradition. The external columns are therefore twice as numerous as they "need" to be, fairly broad, and horizontally grooved to simulate rustication, as in earlier work by Ransome. To see these rusticated piers as the external columns of a frame requires

Minterburn (Roosevelt) Mill, Rockville, Connecticut, by C. R.
Makepeace and Co., 1906. (Photo,
author)

Minterburn Mill, detail of facade.
(Photo, author)

a conscious decision about how to interpret the whole structure, which might be read as a walled system with only an internal frame.

However, it does seem to function structurally as a true monolithic frame, though this does involve some apparent illogicalities in the disposition of the internal members. To achieve a usefully wide spacing between the columns that run down the center of the plan, they are placed at sixteen-foot intervals—which is twice the spacing of the external uprights—so the columns correspond to only every other pier. The beams that span from the exterior to the spine beam carried by the central columns originate at every single upright, and therefore alternate beams have no matching column to accept their inner ends and are supported simply by the mid-section of the spine beam. Since that beam is not visibly deepened to accept this central loading, the result looks awkward, unresolved, and probably improper as an engineering solution. However, I could see no signs of cracking or distortion; the whole structure seems to be in excellent order; and the flat roof does not leak, even during the long snowmelt of the early spring. Like United Shoe Machinery, it excites the admiration of its owner and keepers; it is a very grand old building.

The First Fruits of the New Age

By the end of the critical year of 1906, which saw the two great monuments of transition completed at minterburn and United Shoe Machinery, the three-year intermediate phase was dramatically brought to a close by developments in Detroit and Buffalo, both associated with the name Albert Kahn. In that year two classic automobile manufacturers—a new breed of entrepreneurs with entirely new needs, as it was to turn out—commissioned new manufacturing buildings in concrete: Packard in Detroit, Pierce Arrow in Buffalo. Although there are plenty of other claimants for the design credits for Pierce Arrow, and Kahn's inputs may have been diluted by the ideas of rival engineers, his claim to Packard is clear, since he had been the company's architect from the initiation of work on the new plant on Grand Boulevard in

Packard 10 Building, Detroit, Michigan, by Albert Kahn, 1906. (Photo, author)

Packard 10, detail of facade. (Photo, author)

1903. It is there that one customarily goes to see what Le Corbusier called the "first fruits of the new age," the concrete-framed Daylight factory in its first shamelessly naked purity.

The Packard commission marked the beginning of Albert Kahn's rise as a major figure, first in the fairly small world of Detroit, then nationally. He stepped on to the world stage with his work between 1929 and 1932 on the factories needed by the Soviet regime as, using Ford expertise, they created virtually from scratch a modern automotive industry in Russia. Although Kahn's fame from 1910 onward, after the completion of the first block of the Highland Park Ford plant, was closely linked to the growing legend of Henry Ford and his industrial philosophy, the true basis for the reputation of the Kahn office, and what recommended them to Ford in the first place, was the work at Packard.

As originally conceived by Kahn and the company in 1903, the Packard plant was to be of two-story, brick-pier construction developed around a hollow square occupying the whole of a city block on Grand Boulevard, next to the railroad tracks.[13] This excessively formal plan was never even half executed, however—it can have made little sense operationally or economically—and brick-pier construction had been abandoned within three years of the ground-breaking for the buildings. However, some brick-pier construction, raised to four stories by later additions, survives on the "show facade" toward the boulevard, where it is graced by such traditional usages as rusticated door cases, ornamental tiles, and decorative patterns in the brick bonding, but all subsumed within a properly rational expression of the structural grid.

That facade, however, is the only place in the complex where such graces occur. Having acknowledged some need for conventional architectural decorum on the front, Kahn clearly felt at liberty to dispense with it in the back or anywhere else. The design of the less visible parts of the complex had already reached a kind of architectural null-value condition, stripped of everything but the bare necessities of support and shelter, by the time the epoch-making Building 10 was put in hand. And it is still salutary (if no longer as

George N. Pierce Company (Pierce Arrow), Buffalo, New York, office block, left, by George Cary, 1907–10, and main factory, right, by Lockwood, Greene and Company, 1907 (nearest section). (Photo, Bazelon)

Pierce Arrow, single-story production block, 1907, present state. (Photo, author)

exhilarating as it must once have been) to see the ruthless manner in which Kahn has shrunk everything to this minimal grid of uprights and horizontals, which looks barely adequate to support the production processes. It is not only the number of elements that is minimal, but their cross section and detailing as well.

The inadequacy of the detailing on Building 10 is now very conspicuous. The sharp arrises and exposed corners of the skinny members have spalled off at many points, leaving the corroded reinforcing bars improperly exposed to the weather. Not only is this untidy, but it also contributes to the air of grudging meanness that pervades the whole scheme. What looked so exciting in photographs and magazines seen by European modernists seven thousand miles away, looks cheap and nasty in real life. But it *is* the null-value condition, the zero-term of architecture, and hardly any other architect or builder with a professional conscience could have done it. Few could have brought themselves down (or up?) to this level of cheese-paring economy—or ruthless rationality, if you prefer—even if they had to affect such an attitude to keep the attention of profit-oriented entrepreneurs whom they hoped would commission buildings from their offices.

The extreme position reached so suddenly by Kahn at Packard 10 makes it easy to spot his most likely contributions to Pierce Arrow in Buffalo, where there is again a clearly defined front—in this case a complete office block by the local architect George Cary—that excuses the rest of the buildings from bothering with overt "architecture." The production building is credited to various offices, but no documents among the surviving building permits at city hall give Kahn as architect of title; he is listed only as an associated architect, usually with Lockwood, Greene and Co. as the main designers. What seem to have affixed the name of Kahn to the entire complex were the local passion for attributing everything to the most prestigious names available and the fact that the name of Julius Kahn, of Trussed Concrete, does apply because the firm was the consultant for all the structural aspects.

Anyone who has seen Kahn's work at Packard and knows any comparable buildings by Lockwood, Greene will have little difficulty in attributing the various parts of the plant to their appropriate designers. The detailing of the innovative single-story, monitor-lit production shop and some other structures immediately to its north and west reveals exactly the mean-minded rationality and gracelessness that characterize Packard 10. Nothing else on the site quite has it—certainly not the immensely long block that runs deep down Great Arrow Street on the south side of the complex, built by the Aberthaw Company, in what appears to be a modified Ransome system with projected floor slabs. The work is bare and simple, economical of materials and methods, but it has slightly fatter members and, more importantly, more considered and attentive detailing, such as chamfering the arrises of the columns and beams to protect them against frost spalling, and, following Ransome's recommended practice, to avoid damage when the shuttering was being struck off the concrete.

To my eyes, this is architecture again, if only just. It does go one step beyond the mere provision of safe shelter. Traditional skills appear to have returned, but in some new and chastened forms that have rediscovered the refinements and graces needed to make such minimalizing architecture bearable and workable. The magazine illustrations of such works seen by European modernists were usually too small and too coarse-screened for details as fine as an inch-wide chamfer on the edge of a column to be visible; having never seen the original buildings, they had to discover such usages for themselves, painfully, often too late, and usually at the clients' expense (much as they had with the flat roofs discussed earlier). Such behavior would have been professional suicide for an American industrial architect.

In spite of the revolutionary break with tradition finally wrought by Ransome and Kahn, a vast amount of useful conservative vernacular practice could still be recovered from the former tradition and absorbed back into the new procedures of design. Indeed, it is more than possible that Lockwood, Greene and Co., still based in Boston, may have recovered some of them not only from their own former experience, but also directly from the intermediate East Coast works of Ransome himself, buildings that Kahn may have had no opportunity to see given the comparatively provincial isolation of Detroit. And, to say it again, these were buildings that European radical designers, in the paradoxically metropolitan isolation of Paris, London, Milan, Berlin, St. Petersburg, also had no opportunity to observe. In any case, their lessons on the usefulness of comparative conservatism would probably have been scorned on ideological grounds by the Futurists and members of other modernist combat squads.

In the States, however, the reabsorption of all these good vernacular practices into the new procedures for design and detailing ushered in what can only be described, in art historians' terminology, as a "classic" phase. The "primitive" had been encompassed by the work done down to 1905, or thereabouts; the "late" or "decadent" is typified by Lockwood, Greene's Buffalo Meter building, and lasted from about 1914 until the construction of this type of industrial building was effectively abandoned some time in the twenties. The "mature" or "classic" period thus occupied little over half a decade, but in that short span it bequeathed to many American cities a choice handful of industrial monuments notable for their spare elegance of form and abstinent professionalism of detailing. Those that have not survived unscathed may still exist in fragments large enough, like Kahn's "Old Shop" for Ford at Highland Park, to assure us of the glory that is departed.

To typify the classic glories of that phase, we could hardly do better than to examine the architectural virtues of what is arguably the best building to come from the office of Lockwood, Greene and Co.: the Terminal Warehouse, otherwise the R/S/T building of the Larkin Company, at the eastern extremity of their Seneca Street complex in Buffalo. Though little noticed in the literature on the history of American architecture, it did receive an accolade in the approval of Henry-Russell Hitchcock, who included it in his exhibition of Buffalo Architecture in 1940 and awarded it a high, if peculiarly phrased, place in the local pantheon:

Only in the Larkin warehouse, by a Boston firm, curiously enough, and in George Cary's Pierce Arrow offices, is there any continuation of the line of Wright's industrial architecture.[14]

If "Wright's industrial architecture" means anything of consequence, it can allude to little in built work besides the E-Z Polish factory (built for the Martin brothers, one of whom was Larkin's chief executive) and the Larkin A building, Wright's famous office block for the company. The former was an apparent brick-pier structure, while the Administration building was steel framed, so that, quite apart from their totally different styles, any substantial "line" from them to the concrete-framed R/S/T building would be hard to demonstrate.

In any case, the Larkin Company had deliberately broken the line, partly because of the operational and materials problems they were already experiencing at the Administration building. Nor can one seriously propose any continuation of a Wright line in industrial buildings beyond this point; the next in sequence would be the 1915 A.D. German warehouse in his hometown of Richland Center, Wisconsin. That is a work of considerable interest in its own right: it employs an original form of concrete mushroom construction, and the decoration of the concrete cresting to its blind brick exterior has kept a number of historians busy speculating on its possible sources in pre-Columbian architecture. Its main interest in this study, apart from the concrete work, may be its use of stone basement coursing, almost in the Buffalo mode, under the walls around the loading dock at the rear.

If, on the other hand, Hitchcock is simply talking quality, then the accolade and his remarks are fully justified, for the building is an exceptionally fine one. The quality of the design came from Lockwood, Greene; the equally high quality of the construction came from the Aberthaw Construction Company, also of Boston, which had been founded shortly before expressly to specialize in concrete construction, exploiting patents by Ransome, Kahn, and others. What the Larkin Company wanted was a packing, handling, and shipping facility to accommodate the growth of their enormous mail-order business, a functional program for which the R/S/T block delivers a solution that is both rational and imaginative and is clearly expressed on the exteriors.

This is seen most expressly on the end elevations, whose ten-story height is divided into five functional and structural bays of unequal width, in the sequence: narrow, wide, narrow, wide, narrow. The two wide bays each straddle two lines of railroad tracks, which pass through the full six-hundred-foot length of the warehouse and originally connected with the yards at the back of 701 Seneca. The great length of the facility would enable, at maximum capacity, four average trains of freight cars to load and unload at once. Goods doors at loading docks on the exterior ground-floor walls of the structure meant that materials and merchandise could also be handled via horse-drawn wagons and the gasoline-powered trucks that had already appeared on the streets of Buffalo.

The building is thus intermediate between the Age of the Train and the Age of the Car. It provided for road traffic around its perimeter, but was still enough at the mercy of the high concentrations of activity generated by bulk rail traffic for a traditional tall–long–narrow format to make good operational sense. It seems to introduce a major innovation, however, in standing directly astride the railroad tracks, something that even the operational radicalism of the Ford management did not arrive at until the "New Shop" at Highland Park of 1914–15. But the R/S/T building is still also intermediate in another rather surprising though invisible way: in its mode of reinforcing the concrete. The very complete album of photographs recording the site work during the extraordinarily rapid building campaign of barely six months in the fall and winter of 1910–11 shows a highly unusual form of reinforcement, apparently adopted to speed up construction.[15] It was prefabricated out of flat steel strip and angles, in the form of square open-lattice columns two stories high. Each was lifted in position by crane and bolted

Larkin R/S/T block (Terminal warehouse), Buffalo, New York, by Lockwood, Greene and Company, 1911. (Photo, Bazelon)

Larkin R/S/T under construction. (Photo courtesy Jack Quinan)

to the protruding ends of the section below, which had already been filled with concrete. It was then stayed laterally by horizontal girders to adjacent column frames, and the floor reinforcement was built up on these girders. The pouring of the concrete proceeded conventionally, using the regular kind of wooden formwork and shuttering. Such a procedure is not known to have been used elsewhere, in spite of the economies made possible by transferring much of the work of setting the reinforcement to convenient sites on the ground, rather than to less convenient ones up on the scaffolding.

The building does not clearly fall into any structural category: is it a reinforced concrete structure with unusually substantial reinforcement, or is it a lightweight steel frame with unusually substantial fireproofing? This uncertainty may be appropriate to the times, when "correct" attitudes to concrete design had barely crystallized, but what is astonishing about the building is that there is no uncertainty in the architecture. It is a totally self-assured design, as if architects had been designing in this mode for four centuries, instead of four years! Inside, the huge floors are interrupted only by the widely spaced columns and the elevator stacks (at each end and at one-third and two-thirds of the length) that mark the division into the three separate buildings it constitutes for various legal fictions. The post-and-beam interior frame is also seen on the exterior; indeed, that is all there is to see on the exterior, which is a relentlessly regular grid of concrete uprights and horizontals at regular intervals, interrupted only by the narrower and differently fenestrated bays that correspond to the elevator stacks. These breaks may be all that save the facades from utter monotony when viewed in their entirety, but what lifts the design from the tolerable to the noble is the quality of the detailing of the expressed structure. In the conventional uses of the term, there is no "detailing" whatsoever at R/S/T, but everywhere one looks there is evidence of great care and ingenious thought in dealing with edges and corners, junctions and relationships of materials, and the proportioning of the whole. The lowest floor, as is customary, is a good third higher than those

Larkin R/S/T, end elevation. (Photo, Bazelon)

Larkin R/S/T, main facade system.
(Photo, Bazelon)

Larkin R/S/T, interior at completion.
(Photo courtesy Jack Quinan)

Larkin R/S/T, detailing of concrete
and brickwork. (Photo, Bazelon)

above—freight cars are taller than people—and is pierced by the door openings of the loading docks. One or two of the original wooden up-and-over doors survive, but most have been replaced; the steel-plate details of the sills and transoms of these openings are still in place, however, as are the angle irons on the jambs, installed to protect the bricks from being chipped by the swinging doors of trucks and carts and other daily accidents. These are all usages that can be found in the Reidpath designs on the rest of the Larkin site, and it is a tribute to the ability of the Lockwood, Greene design team that they have made these elements of the former tradition look equally at home on their radically different structure.

On the nine regular floors above, the detailing is consistent; the frame itself is totally flat-faced and rectangular in section, but the exposed arrises of the uprights, which stand slightly proud of the horizontals, have the proper chamfered edges to protect them against spalling. The openings of the frame are infilled quite simply by a low spandrel or apron of red brickwork, pierced by a drainage scupper and topped by a plain concrete sill, carrying (where the originals survive) three sashes of regular industrial double-hung wooden glazing. Such window framing was entirely conventional for its time; and where an area of several bays and floors of it have survived together, as on the north side of the block, one can see how the change of color, close rhythm, and moderate projections of the wooden glazing bars have enriched and enlivened the surface of the facade.

One might propose the glazing bars as the least term in a series of systematically related members and dimensions, whose appropriate combinations account for the unarguable elegance and proprotionable congruence of the whole. Of course the fact that there is practically nothing but elegance of proportions to be seen leaves the viewer little else to ponder, since everything but these few neat details has been stripped away. Even so, there is no sign here of the miserliness of Kahn's work at Packard 10; the margins of difference, however, are almost unbelievably slight. Besides mystical qualities such as the "immanent presence of genius," or whatever one likes to call it, they seem to be: the fatter visible columns required by the greater height, the softening effect of chamfered edges, the excellent and very regular bricklaying, and standard bay dimensions that happily add up to a very gratifying set of proportional relations. One other matter must be noted, in all fairness; Packard, though still occupied and used, appears to have had no serious maintenance since the original company quit business almost a quarter of a century ago, whereas R/S/T has been restored and maintained in exemplary condition by its present occupiers, Graphic Controls Inc.

The building looks so good that it inevitably sets the standard by which other and more famous buildings of the period may be judged. Ford's Old Shop at Highland Park, for instance, still Kahn's most celebrated work, is just not in the same class though it is of exactly the same generation as a design-concept. Nothing, of course, can take away its historical significance; its close association with Henry Ford's most notable product, the mass-produced Model T, the car that proverbially put the world on wheels, guarantees it a place in the history of Western civilization, while the fact that it was illustrated in Gropius's *Jahrbuch* article and was the avowed inspiration of Matte-Trucco's Fiat factory in Turin ensures its place in the present study. Yet it seems that it must be judged something of a functional failure, not through any fault of its own, but because of the pace of innovation in production techniques at Ford in the period immediately following its completion at the end of 1909. The well-known photograph of the body-to-chassis rig occupying most of the height of several bays outside the back of the block, though now known to represent an experimental hook-up and not standard operating procedure, nevertheless gives one a fair idea of the kind of thinking about production methods that was going on at Ford. Such multi-story concepts could not be fitted into a structure like the Old Shop, with its regular monolithic floor slabs.

This may be one of the reasons why the New Shop is two stories higher than the old (against the grain of Ford's later thinking, as exemplified by the single-story sheds of the

River Rouge plant) and has aisles, rising the full height of the block, that offer the convenience of bringing the railroad tracks right through the building. However, the Old Shop continued to serve the company in various capacities until its demolition in 1959 and thus demonstrated that remarkable adaptability of use—due to the standardized, wide, open loft spaces of the interior—which this generation of factories also inherited from the former tradition. Such adaptability was to be lost in subsequent generations as the structures and spaces came to be more tightly tailored to their specified functions.

The architecture of the Old Shop was also, I found, something of a disappointment. It was not completely demolished in 1959, as is often implied, and a substantial section, some fifteen bays long, survives partially behind the former Lincoln office block. It lacks the ruthlessness of the design of Packard 10, even at the back, and the stylish, naked elegance of R/S/T at the front, but the fact that the architecture is visibly different front and back appears to indicate a particular problem which, I suspect, may even have been of Kahn's own making. The Old Shop was not just a production facility; with its immensely long facade running parallel with Woodward Avenue for a whole city block and clearly visible in spite of three smaller structures in front, it was also part of the public face of Ford. It therefore had to be "architecture," as the term would be understood by Kahn and Edward Grey (his collaborator inside the company).

Ford Old Shop, Highland Park, Detroit, Michigan, by Albert Kahn and Edward Grey, 1908. (From *Jahrbuch des Deutschen Werkbundes*, 1913; courtesy Avery Library, Columbia University)

Alling and Corry Building, Buffalo,
New York, by R. J. Reidpath and
Son, 1910. (Photo, Bazelon)

Alling and Corry, cornice detail.
(Photo, Bazelon)

The Daylight Factory   99

Ford Old Shop, Highland Park; present condition of northern end.
(Photo, author)

Ford Old Shop; surviving facade toward Woodward Avenue. (Photo,
author)

Its businesslike and technically advanced steel-sash glazing was therefore framed in brick cladding over the concrete frame, and the junctions of columns and beams were accentuated by decorative ceramic tiles. The four-story facade is crowned by a simplified modillion cornice and interrupted by towers with comparatively ornate crestings; to modern eyes this is no improvement on the unadorned rear facade. Even among its contemporaries with classicizing framed structures and cornices, it hardly bears comparison with, say, the remarkably elegant and accomplished Alling and Corry building in Buffalo, designed by the Reidpath office, which is a close cousin to the now vanished Alling and Corry building in Cincinnati, illustrated by Gropius in the *Jahrbuch*. Kahn, it seems to me, did better in one way in his conventional architecture, as on the campus at Ann Arbor, and better in another way in the sequence of enormous steel-framed single-story sheds for the automotive and aircraft industries that begins with the Ford plant at River Rouge and continues to the 1940s.

And yet . . . to stand in the litter-filled forecourt of what remains of the Old Shop, under the shadow of Kahn's show facade, and look down the long wilderness of broken bricks and concrete rubble that was the site of the rest of it, stretching for hundreds of feet down toward Manchester Avenue, and then to consider what was wrought here in the peak years of Henry Ford's creativity, is still impressive—if only for what it has to tell us of the transience of industrial fame and the buildings that enshrined it. As Grant Hildebrand observed in his excellent book on the work of Albert Kahn:

Interesting as it was, this approach to the housing of manufacturing was soon to be outmoded with Ford's introduction in this same plant of the powered moving assembly line. Within five years of the opening of Highland Park, Henry Ford would turn his thoughts to a new manufacturing complex, and within seven years the company would embark on a policy of one-story buildings to the virtual exclusion of the multistory scheme.[16]

The wonder, now, must be that a building doomed to such early obsolescence should have been permitted to stand for half a century and finally perish only in 1959. Such reflections can only make us grateful that so many (small though the total roster may be) of the buildings of this classic period have survived long enough to demonstrate to us that the radical pursuit of the economic rationalities of capitalist enterprise did not necessarily or on every occasion lead to a merely instrumental meanness and lack of grace. But then neither the Ford, Larkin, nor Buffalo Meter companies were simply dominated by a conventional lust for profits alone. Some other objective was also in view, some larger vision, even some humane sense of social responsibility, and so the old connection between good architecture and intelligent patronage clearly continued, even in the apparently relentless pursuit of "the bottom line." The romantically tough-minded beliefs of many European modernists that the American engineers were "not in pursuit of an architectural idea, but guided simply by the necessities of an imperative demand," as Le Corbusier phrased it, must be taken with a grain of salt; what can only be interpreted as architectural ideas were clearly being pursued, or even carried forward from the former tradition and other more traditional sources, and much of the power and conviction of the work that was admired in the second and third decades of the century or survives for us to admire today, comes from those old ingrained professional habits of both builders and designers.

Afterthought: Frames of Reference
Those readers who have been surprised to see a large and crucial period of the development of modern American industry discussed without the conventional references to labor history and sociology—no strikes, no Taylorism, no mention of Henry Ford's "Five Dollar Day"—are probably less alarmed than readers brought up on the "authorized version" of the history of modern architecture, as advanced by, say, Sigfried Giedion or as understood by many school-trained architects practicing in North America, one of whom encapsulated it for me thus, while he was still a student: "I always understood that modern architecture started in Chicago and was caused by the electric elevator and the steel frame."

To find the history of the "pioneer" period of modern architecture discussed without reference to the rise of the skyscraper in Chicago, with almost no references to the steel frame or Louis Sullivan, and early concrete work discussed with no more than passing references to the likes of Auguste Perret, François Hennebique, and Eugene Freyssinet may well seem narrow-minded or even bizarrely provincial. These have long been established as great names and great themes in the rise of modern architecture, yet in the present study, which looks at yet another great theme in that history, they seem hardly relevant at all. If one checks the illustrations to the article by Gropius that stirred the theme in the first place, one will find only one factory that may have had a steel frame (Continental Motors in Detroit) and only two grain elevators (the Dakota in Buffalo, Government 1 in Montreal) that can definitely be identified as steel-built, and in neither case was that steel "expressed" in the manner supposed to be fundamental to modern architecture. And among Le Corbusier's imagery in *Vers une Architecture* there are, under the rubric "Surface," as far as one can tell from such badly reproduced half-tones, no illustrations at all of steel-framed factories. These issues, so often central to narratives of the rise of modern architecture, are fairly marginal here.

This is not to say that either Gropius or Le Corbusier were ignorant of, say, Louis Sullivan, whose myth as a great misunderstood genius and master of modernism seems to have been current in Europe even before 1914, presumably due to the presence in 1910 of Frank Lloyd Wright, to whom the Sullivan myth was to become so important. But whether as myth or fact, Sullivan had no relevance to the arguments of Gropius about industrial architecture, while the relentless ornamentalism of the surfaces of his buildings would surely have made him anathema to Le Corbusier's purist sensibility and was precisely the kind of thing that led him to warn his readers to "beware of American architects." Without wishing to propose that the work of architects like Sullivan and Wright had only a marginal influence on the rise of modern architecture in Europe, a rereading of the literature suggests that the large and honorable place allotted to them, their virtual co-option into the history of European modernism, is a scholastic maneuver of writers of the thirties. One might even argue that the influence of the architects of Chicago was far less than that of the illustrations of industrial buildings in other cities.

The matter of the rise of the industrial concrete frame, however, is more substantial and merits closer attention. How far removed could it be from the rise of the steel frame, and how independent could the American developments in concrete be of those in Europe? It could not, I suspect, be entirely independent of the rise of the skyscraper, whether in Chicago or New York, because it is highly unlikely that men as shrewd and observant as Heidenreich, Turner, or Ransome would fail to note what was happening in an adjoining field, any more than they would be ignorant of European work in concrete, since the patents were on file in the United States. There were, of course a few relatively tall—if hardly skyscraping—buildings in reinforced concrete in the period under review; Gropius illustrates one of them, the Roth Packing Company warehouse in Cincinnati. In the same city was the sixteen-story Ingalls building of 1903, for which Elzner and Anderson were the architects, but which seems to have been put together largely out of the standard kit of parts of the Ransome Patent System.

In general, though, the two cultures of steel and concrete seem to have been remarkably independent of one another. If one may judge from what is printed in the pages of, say, *Engineering News* in the first decade of this century, steel-framed construction was not seen as a topic of great interest to the readership, in spite of the large amount of it that was still going up. This is hardly surprising; the heroic and innovating phase of steel framing could be seen as virtually over by 1895 or so, and work in that material might be judged routine and unchallenging by the brighter young engineers of the period. Both Heidenreich and Turner, for instance, appear to have been perfectly capable engineers in steel, but the reputation of neither depended on accomplishments in that field. Concrete, on the other hand, was clearly the exciting new material at the turn of the century, and its use, as measured by the quantity of cement consumed, is reckoned to have increased some fifteen-hundred fold in the United States between 1880 and 1910!

Also, for reasons connected with fireproofing, concrete soon became the material *par excellence* for the construction of factories—and for very little else. Indeed, for many applications, particularly of a "representational" kind, it was still commonly regarded as an inferior or improper material, so one salutes Jane Lathrop Stanford's insistence on its use at the campus that bears her family's name, even if the results, despite Ransome's engineering skill, hardly do architectural honor to that name. There were powerful interests still trying to keep concrete out of "proper" architecture, even after the San Francisco earthquake had demonstrated its strength. Unlike steel, it did not necessarily require facing, a consideration that paradoxically led the masonry trades to favor steel over concrete.[17]

More than this, however, a deep gulf of either indifference or incomprehension between the cultures of steel and concrete is strongly suggested by the curiously oblique way in which Ernest Ransome came at his invention of the concrete frame: projecting the edge of the floor slab beyond the outer row of columns and then cutting off what protruded, so to speak, rather than simply taking over the idea from the more-or-less isotropic grids of the steel frames of buildings he must have seen going up in New York and elsewhere. It is very difficult to believe that so intelligent a man would not have seen the relevance of the one to the other, unless there were some real obstacles of professional habit or specialization.

This seems to be confirmed by the apparent failure of any of his younger colleagues to come up with the framed solution any earlier than he did. The idea was just not in the subculture that went with concrete, nor was the idea of borrowing it from other practices. But then, most of his contemporaries or juniors in Europe missed the solution also. For this general failure one can probably offer a fairly straightforward technical explanation. A grid needs horizontal beams as well as uprights, and beams had long been a structurally dubious proposition in reinforced concrete until good and necessary procedures (intellectual and physical) for locating the reinforcing bars in the depth of the beam and for preventing structurally damaging slippage between the concrete and the reinforcement had been worked out. A flurry of inventions and patents on both sides of the Atlantic and either side of the year 1900 finally resolved these problems and ushered in the era of precisely calculated beams. Without such beams economical frame structures in concrete were unthinkable.

Around 1900, then, the action and the excitement were not in iron and steel but in concrete, which was about to take off into the most spectacular stage of its development in the United States. The new men, headed by Ransome, were above all specialists in concrete, and their subject matter—the Daylight factory and the grain elevator—was to be (along with bridge building) concrete's primary province. The evidence for this is overwhelming, on the ground and in the professional literature. Why, then, has this development been so largely overlooked, as much in histories of American modernism by American writers as by European authors of works on modernism in general?

The answers appear to lie in two clearly dominant trends in much of the standard literature on modern architecture: one may be called the Primacy Rule, the other is the Metropolitan Viewpoint. The Primacy Rule means that in the eyes of many historians it is more important to have done something first than to have done something good or useful with it. It may indeed stimulate the sporting interests of academics to hunt down the first use of "structural steel" or "concrete," even if the heat and enthusiasm of the hunt lead them to force strange meanings on those words. What influences the practical constructors who put up the buildings that eventually become the monuments that constitute the built history of architecture, however, is to see a useful building that works, in some way, better than buildings made of other or earlier materials. In the history of concrete construction, then, the older building at Bayonne for Pacific

Coast Borax, by surviving the fire of 1902, may be the most important structure in reinforced concrete in North America.

However, the reason why it seems to have gone largely unobserved is almost certainly that it would have been very difficult to observe from any academic viewpoint (even if, as seems very likely, the glow of the flames was visible from the heights of the Columbia campus in New York!). The general history of reinforced concrete and its effect on modern architecture is dominated by the names of Perret, Freyssinet, and Hennebique because this history has been written mostly by European academics like Sigfried Giedion and Nikolaus Pevsner. It is almost a matter of the very geography of Western culture—whatever happened in Paris or Berlin or London was perceived to be important, New York almost as much so, and Chicago could not be gainsaid because of the manifest genius of Frank Lloyd Wright, which made it necessary to bracket into the argument his predecessors like Louis Sullivan. But who ever heard of Cincinnati, Minneapolis, Bayonne, Buffalo, Oakland, Montreal, Duluth . . . even somewhere as conspicuous in the history of modern manufacturing technology as Detroit?

This invisibility of the provinces is the more remarkable because the high esteem accorded one or two select provincial pioneers of modern architecture—Antoni Gaudi in Barcelona, Charles Rennie Mackintosh in Glasgow, for instance—should have alerted historians to the fact that the prime activities in architecture and building around the turn of the century were less likely to be in the metropolitan cities than in provincial commercial centers. To discuss the rise of the concrete frame without giving proper consideration to all the contributors is to deprive the provinces of their due, to overlook the work of some highly talented designers, and to ignore some remarkable buildings whose presence truly enriches our view of the architecture of the twentieth century. And that—as this book is here to argue—is to mislay some of the true sources of the International Style, which will remain, as far as anyone can yet see, the dominant style of the high art of architecture in the twentieth century.

Colossal utilitarian architecture of great form may also come into being in spheres of civilization poor in myths.

Wilhelm Worringer, Egyptian Art

2

The Grain Elevator

The Mechanical System

As a building type, the classic form of grain elevator so much admired by architects of the modern movement does not have as long or substantial a prehistory in any tradition as does the Daylight factory. The characteristic format of cylindrical bins, head-houses, lofting legs, and so on had barely emerged by the end of the nineteenth century, largely because the materials were not there to build it in those shapes. What prehistory the type does have is chiefly the evolution of the mechanical system to move the grain in and out of the storage bins. What makes an elevator an elevator is not that it occupies a particular building form, but that it has machinery for raising the grain to the top of the storage vessels.

As long as the human race has eaten grain products, it has been faced with the problem of storing them. That problem was resolved by the use of closed vessels, such as baskets or pots, usually the bigger the better for economy. But beyond a certain size, such vessels became too heavy to lift or tip, and the business of extracting the grain from them required the use of smaller vessels, such as ladles or scoops. The active part of a grain elevator consists of machinery for tipping or scooping grain from farm carts, freight cars, or the holds of ships into the storage bins and decanting it later into other forms of transport (or, occasionally, directly into a milling plant). Various mechanisms now exist for performing these operations, but in the period when the grain elevator was effectively invented, the best device was the bucket conveyor: a series of scoops affixed to a belt or chain which passed over two end pulleys or sprockets, the lower one buried in the grain in the vessel to be emptied and the other one, at the upper end of the "leg," positioned above the vessel to be filled or above a hopper whose outflow could be directed into an appropriate vessel by means of a chute. As an engine rotated the sprockets, the buckets on the chain each bit into the grain in turn as they passed under the lower sprocket and discharged it as they tipped over in rounding the upper one. Such technology was not at all common in the period preceding the invention of the grain elevator in 1843 by Joseph Dart of Buffalo, and he seems most likely to have picked up the idea from his acquaintance Oliver Evans, whose proposal for a gravity-fed grain mill indicated such a bucket conveyor as the means for raising grain to storage bins at the top of the plant, whence it could flow down under its own weight through the sequence of milling processes. Dart's peculiar problem, which did not affect Evans's invention, was to devise a means of lowering the bottom end of the bucket chain into the holds of the large vessels that brought grain across the Great Lakes or of the barges that moved it along the Erie Canal.

The previous technology for unloading these boats gave no clues for solving this problem, since it consisted simply of teams of stevedores (unreliable and drunk, or so Buffalo remembers them) ascending and descending a series of ladders, from ship's hold to wharf level and from wharf level to the tops of bins, carrying the grain on their backs and discharging it into the bins. The new technology was an assembly of mechanisms already to hand: the bucket conveyor, the steam engine, rope-and-pulley power trains, and the like. The most crucial features of Dart's invention were that it, first, eliminated the intermediate handling stage at wharf level and raised the grain directly to the tops of the bins by, second, using a rigid, nearly vertical frame to carry the bucket, chain, and sprocket assembly. The frame could be raised and lowered as a complete unit by means of a cradle of ropes and pulleys whose winches were powered by the same steam engine as drove the bucket conveyor. In a later improvement, further power from the steam engine was tapped by another set of winches pulling ropes attached to large wooden scoops that were used to drag loose grain across the floor of the ship's hold and into the jaws of the conveyor. This complete, independently powered assembly, if contained in a building of its own, was (and still is, where it survives) identified as a "marine tower" or more familiarly as a "leg"; in Buffalo, at least, it was known as a "stiff" leg if permanently built into the storage structure or a "loose" leg if movable. Early versions of the loose leg were mounted on their own barges or floats and were used for transferring grain between floating vessels. This type remained in use in many ports until after 1900 and can be seen in old photographs—tall, pyramidal wood-clad structures wrapped in the steam and smoke from their own power plants.

This was also the only version that could be described simply as an "elevator," uncluttered by nonmechanical functions such as storage. The fact that this image is so much less familiar—to architects in particular—than that of a massive storage structure standing on the water's edge or isolated in the wastes of a flat prairie landscape is the consequence of another, and almost completely separate, story of structural and mechanical development, which eventually gave to European modernists the set of admired images they tended to describe rather indiscriminately as "elevators" or "silos." The beginnings of that story are remote and vernacular: as far as the pictorial evidence can be read, it seems to show Dart's pioneering leg built on to the front of a fairly conventional wooden shed with a pitched roof, within which the storage bin or bins were located —another *ad hoc* combination of functional elements that were already to hand.

The same is true of other early elevators in the Buffalo area and elsewhere, but as the grain trade grew toward the end of the century, the need for ever larger storage vessels soon created a situation where the bins or cribs became the dominant parts of the installation, and the building envelopes

City A and B Elevators, Buffalo,
New York, after 1880 (both de-
stroyed 1908). (From Severance, A
Picture Book of Earlier Buffalo, 1912)

Bennett Elevator, Buffalo, New
York, after 1880 (destroyed 1912).
(From Severance, A Picture Book of
Earlier Buffalo, 1912)

were made—effectively if not conceptually—by simply roofing and cladding the bins, their headworks, and the "house" containing the bulk of the elevating machinery. Such structures could be very handsome in a stern, no-nonsense way; old photographs of the Bennett elevator, which stood from the eighties until demolished in 1912, show a plain and apparently well-made structure of tall, thin section, with a fairly steeply pitched gable roof, arched openings at ground level, and a kind of pedimented extension in the center of its flat facade to serve as the house for the machinery. It had a chimney stack for the steam engine that powered the leg, which descended from, and could be retracted into, a sort of projecting oriel on the front.

That this particular elevator should have stood so long— around thirty years—suggests that it was not only better designed than most of its contemporaries, but also very much better built. The average life of a wood and brick elevator was reckoned to be around twelve to fifteen years, not because of obsolescence or structural decay, but because of fire or explosion. Not only was the internal construction inherently flammable—wooden bins, stairs, floors, ladders, chutes for the grain—but atmospheres heavily laden with grain dust could also be disastrously explosive in the presence of sparks, which had many potential sources, from lamps and the steam engines to friction in moving parts that were inadequately lubricated.

The search for a more fireproof form of construction, preferably an *inexpensive* form, was clearly the main motive behind the many experiments with different materials and structural procedures which marked the nineties and the first decade or so of the present century. While these convulsions in the building of the storage bins were going on, however, change in the mechanical plant was slower, though in the end no less significant. The forms and operation of the legs could hardly change, though toward the end of the nineties electrical power introduced a new freedom in the disposition of the legs in relation to the bins. Liberated from the restrictions on transmitting power over long distances by means of shafting and belts, electrically powered legs could be multiplied in number or, given suitable sliding or rolling power pick-ups, could be made to move on rails, so that the "loose" legs could come ashore. Either way, a greater number of legs could simultaneously service the same number of bins and/or boats. In this they were aided by a purely mechanical development that immediately made much bigger installations possible: horizontal transfer conveyors (with either rubber belts or, earlier, archimedean screws) that could move the grain along above the bins for input and below them for output—usually with the addition of internal "lofting" legs for the transfer of grain from the lower to the upper systems of horizontal conveyors. These last mechanical developments also had an effect on the form of the installations since an economical use of such horizontal transfers, known as the Chase system, required that the bins be ranked in straight rows; the evolution of the long, high, narrow elevator complexes of the early twentieth century can be traced back to this change in handling processes. The long form also suited the use of rail-mounted loose legs, which could patrol along the front of a continuous, straight row of bins more easily than if the bins were disposed in any other pattern.

One thing that electricity could not do was eliminate the risk of fire or explosion caused by sparks, although enclosed switches, improved motors, and better design derived from accumulated experience (and pressure from insurance companies!) gradually reduced the risks. In any case, as the risk of fire slowly diminished, it became increasingly clear that there were other threats to the safety and stability of elevators and silos, derived from the behavior of grain in bulk. It can behave almost like a solid at some times, almost like a liquid at others, and the change of state can be extremely sudden. Even in the open holds of ships, let alone in more restricted locations, these changes can look almost catastrophic. I have watched a twelve-foot cliff of red durum wheat in the hold of a Steinbrenner ship in the Buffalo River, standing at what was clearly steeper than its natural angle of repose, suddenly let go and flow like a wave around the legs of the men working in the hold. Had the flow been deeper, it could have toppled a standing man. Old hands in the trade know when to stand out from under, but I could now understand the piteous tales I used to hear about inexperienced lads being buried and suffocated under falls of grain.

Most of the problems and threats to structures, however, stem from grain's static "liquid" behavior. Like a liquid in a tank, it exerts outward pressure on the side walls of the bins; this is the reason usually given for the relatively shallow bins of many early elevators and granaries, since that form would ensure that the load was taken mostly as dead weight on the floors of the bins rather than as bursting pressure against the walls. Such broad bins were clearly wasteful of premium ground space at the wharf, so taller bins were desirable, and a way of making them more resistant to bursting pressures was therefore sought. The first solution, using wooden construction, was to appear in the 1870s: the so-called cribbed bin, whose rectangular walling was built up of layers of large planks laid flat and then spiked together, layer by layer, with massive nails. Such construction was rigid enough to resist not only bursting pressure, but also its reverse, the sudden vacuums that could develop if the grain began to flow suddenly while being emptied under gravity through ports at the bottom of the bin.

Clearly, what was needed to solve these mechanical problems was a material of high tensile strength, fireproofing performance, and a structural geometry that would put the tensile strength to work while being self-bracing to resist sudden vacuums. A model for the geometry was at hand throughout the industrialized world, used with at least one fairly suitable material: it was the regular steam boiler, or storage tank for liquids, built up out of riveted steel plate and cylindrical in form so that bursting loads were taken up as pure tension in the outer skin. In strict mathematical terms, of course, a sphere would have been even stronger and have an even better ratio of enclosed volume to exterior surface, but in practice would have been too difficult to fabricate and ridiculously expensive. For the simple storage of liquids or near liquids, however, where there is no vertical thrust against the top of the container, a cylinder

Standard Elevator, Buffalo, New York, showing "marine legs" at work. (Photo, Bazelon)

standing on end is structurally sound (or should be) and has a quite respectable volume-to-surface ratio. Although the occasional construction of cylindrical steel or wrought-iron boilerplate tanks for grain storage appears to date back to the 1860s, when George H. Johnson built something of the sort in Brooklyn and Philadelphia,[1] there seems to have been little enthusiasm for this type of construction in the trade until the very end of the century. The slow adoption of the steel-tank bin, one may guess, had four main causes beyond an unfamiliarity that is supposed to have produced an almost superstitiously irrational aversion to Johnson's pioneer examples: the comparatively high cost of the material and the specialized skills required to fabricate it (riveting boilerplate is a very different matter from spiking planks together); rust and corrosion; steel's poor performance as a thermal insulator; and lastly the geometrical problems of packing circular bins into a rectangular building without leaving a lot of wasteful and awkwardly shaped spaces between them.

One attempted solution to these problems can be seen in a set of elevators of heroic scale that went up just after 1895. All were designed by Max Toltz, the bridge builder and presiding engineering genius of the golden age of the Great Northern Railway, which served Minnesota and the western Great Lakes area. One of them was in Duluth, Minnesota; one in West Superior, Wisconsin; and the third was at the other end of the lake-shipping trade, at Buffalo, New York. All were enormous, with capacities of better than two million bushels, and were housed in brick shells of handsome architectural aspect. They also produced a spate of awed rhetoric in the pages of *Engineering News* in 1901:

The great increase in the capacity and mechanical equipment of grain elevators, combined with the substitution of steel for timber in their construction, have placed these structures among the most important engineering works of modern times. Perhaps one of the best, and certainly one of the latest examples of elevator construction which deserve mention, is the 3,000,000 bushel terminal elevator put in operation at West Superior, Wis., in February of this year. This elevator was built by the Great Northern Railway and is designed to eclipse in every way the mammoth steel elevator built by the same company at Buffalo, New York, in 1897–98.[2]

The West Superior version had 505 bins packed within its brick walls. They were indeed made of steel but were square in plan, so that they gained the spatial economies of close packing, but sacrificed the full structural performance of a cylindrical format, though they obviously retained the fireproofing qualities. The slightly earlier version in Buffalo (known as the Great Northern), however, had cylindrical bins, and its mode of dealing with the resulting problems of economy of space and internal transfer of grain make it one of the most remarkable buildings in the present study.

By the time my students and I came to know the Great Northern, the Pillsbury Company was employing it as a storage and blending facility for their Buffalo flour-milling plant, which was in an adjoining structure. With only one or two exceptions, the elevators still operational in Buffalo by the end of the 1970s survived only as adjuncts to mills, and Pillsbury closed even the Great Northern in 1982. Externally it is a huge brown brick box, the equivalent of ten regular stories high and long to match, at just over three hundred feet. Since it was a "terminal" elevator, used for transferring waterborne grains at the railhead, it was equipped with two loose legs, clad in corrugated iron—which was almost a "timeless" material in this particular context, since it was used on all generations of legs surviving in Buffalo by then. In elevators this size, the legs were the equivalent of a nine-story tower-block but were capable of moving along the tracks under their own power. Such displacement was slow and ponderous, rather than excitingly rapid, but one cannot help feeling that European modernists who admired the elevators so much would have been fired to even greater enthusiasm had they known that large parts—*very* large parts—of these buildings could move about the Earth's surface in this way. Since the towers containing these legs were rarely as much as twenty feet square in plan and the wheeled trolleys on which they ran projected little beyond that dimension, their stability was marginal. When operating, rather than moving, the legs were locked down to the rails with clamps, but even so their upright stance could be perilous. The loose legs that I saw at the Great Northern are a replacement pair, tied back to the building itself by sprung restraints running on a rail near the top of the wall on that side. The previous set, without such restraints, had been toppled by a gale in the 1930s and fallen athwart a grain ship moored to the wharf.

The landward side of the Great Northern is uncluttered by such equipment and still demonstrates the sheer artistry of the industrial brickwork of the former tradition at its late best—a pure wall, almost uninterrupted by openings and barely modeled by the necessities of buttressing and corbeling. Yet this "almighty wall" carries none of the weight of the internal storage system and little of that of the headworks. It is a pure weatherproofing skin, and the closure of the box against the elements is completed by a low-pitched roof whose central part suddenly rises in a steep clerestory that must, one realizes from counting the superimposed ranges of regular industrial windows, be as tall as a four-story building.

Inside this vast box, a chassis of substantial, vertical, eighteen-inch built-up steel I-beams carries the forty-eight main cylindrical steel bins that fill the interior. With the assistance of thirty minor cylinders that are packed into the spaces between the main bins and those between the bins and the

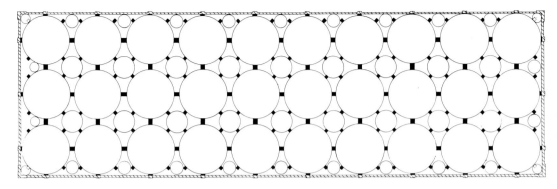

Great Northern Elevator, plan of
bins. (Drawn by Donald Theurer)

Great Northern Elevator, ground
floor. (Photo, Bazelon)

outer walls, the box is so tightly packed with bins that the elevator to the work floors in the head-house had to be specially shaped to fit the leftover space in one corner of the box. The only view from inside the open cage is of a continuous curved face of well-assembled steel boilerplate passing a few inches from one's face.

The bins do not come down to the ground; the chassis supports their deep conical bottoms well above an open floor, and from their bottoms extend tubular chutes that can be swivelled to discharge into pits in the floor, from which internal lofting legs carry the grain to the top of the head-works, whence it can be redistributed to other bins during blending operations. The conical bin bottoms, lofting legs, oblique chutes, and the legs of the chassis, seen together, seem like a gigantic surrealist architecture turned upside down or like the abandoned cathedral of some sect of iron men. Weird as this may sound, it is a highly impressive space, monumental in scale and in the quality of the work, and that is a rare experience in the world of grain elevators, which are not usually, nor need be, provided with anything like public spaces. The head-house too is almost cathedral-like: long, lit by ranks of industrial windows in the corrugated roofing on either side, filled with a golden-gray atmosphere of flying grain dust sliced by low shafts of sunlight. The space is laced lengthwise by flat rubber belt conveyors loaded with grain and laced diagonally by more movable chutes for directing the flow of grain. Weigh bins over the heads of the main bins measure the flow, batch by batch, as it goes from bin to bin. The whole is monitored by men who watch steelyards connected to the weigh bins and mounted on desks whose legs are in the form of short cast-iron Doric columns—a touch I particularly enjoyed, since the use of Doric columns as supports for mechanical or scientific equipment was a piece of "typical" early-Victorian stylistic impropriety much abused by the propagandists of the modern movement in architecture when I was a lad!

This then is a grand old monument to an intermediate phase of the rise of modern industrial architecture in the United States. It is comparable in scale to other intermediate

Great Northern Elevator, main floor
of head-house. (Photo, Bazelon)

monuments, like the United Shoe Machinery plant, but in its great eclecticism of materials and construction techniques, it has more in common with the last stages of the former tradition, as exemplified by the old Keystone workshop on Chandler Street. Unlike these last two designs, however, it offers no clues to further development; it stands at the end of the line that had started with the simple shed of Joseph Dart's first elevator—a building filled with bins. As is overwhelmingly clear when one confronts them, such works have their own monumentality, nobility, and strength; but they did not catch the eye of Gropius or his American contacts, despite his professed admiration for these qualities. One intermediate steel-framed elevator in Buffalo does appear among his illustrations, however: the Dakota, designed by the seemingly omnicompetent Reidpath office to replace a wood-cribbed elevator that had burned down in 1906, and destroyed in its turn in the 1960s to make way for the overhead section of the New York thruway. The Dakota was in many ways a freak—innovative but stuck in its own time. It had steel bins in a steel chassis but no external brick skin. Nearly all its ancillary activities were housed in a broad head-house so large that it projected on either side beyond the bins below, giving it a "hammerhead" silhouette that is certainly striking—but has nothing to do with the spectacular and radical direction in which elevator design had already begun to move.

Forms Assembled in the Light
The solution to the problem of packing circular bins into rectangular buildings without wasteful leftover spaces was obvious but was so radical that it clearly was not thinkable for some time: discarding the building and letting the bins stand out in the open air, though it would deprive the contents of a layer of weatherproofing. This was ultimately to be the solution whatever the material from which the bins were constructed, but by a margin of a very few years, it was done with steel bins before brick, tile, or concrete. It had been tried in Buffalo even before the Great Northern was built, but even in the 1970s the pioneering installation—the Electric Elevator, later the Cargill-Electric—was still

seen by some old hands along Childs Street, where it stood among a regular museum of historic elevators, as a rather second-rate, cut-price affair, and the complaint, chiefly, was its poor thermal insulation as compared to brick-clad structures. The issue was not so much freezing in the winter cold as the problems that arose in the heat of summer, when the stored grain had to be turned much too frequently to prevent sprouting, the incubation of bacterial infestations, or the formation of dangerous hot spots that could cause explosions. How seriously one should take these criticisms is not clear; the constant turning of grain is a profitless use of plant and would be unlikely to recommend itself to operators. Although naked steel-bin elevators were built for only a short period around and after 1900, some are still in use, which indicates that their shortcomings cannot be as serious as reputation suggests. The early demise of steel, against the weight of expert opinion in the magazines that it was the most suitable material, must be laid to other causes.

The classics of the steel epoch were the Pioneer Steel Elevator of 1901; the slightly later Electric Steel Elevator, in Minneapolis; and the Electric Elevator in Buffalo, which preceded them by some five years. Less good looking to some eyes, the latter has the very considerable distinction of being the first elevator to be electrically powered and therefore the first, also, to be equipped with a mobile loose leg.

If not handsome, the Electric, in its almost ninety years on the edge of the Buffalo River (it was demolished in 1984), acquired a certain grimy conviction about its forms; their functionality was as strikingly manifest as the technical innovations that underlie the design. On the wharf side, it presented a weird, original, and drastically simplified architecture in black corrugated iron. The head-house cum workshed was very much wider than deep and rather tall, the impression of height being accentuated by the flush surfaces and vertical corrugations of the cladding. The latter was interrupted only by small and strategically located windows of a more-wide-than-high format at variance with all other Buffalo practice in the metal-clad parts of elevators. On the front of the house were two modest projecting

Pioneer Steel Elevator, Minneapolis,
Minnesota, by The Barnett and
Record Company, 1901. (Photo,
Bazelon).

Cargill ("Electric") Elevator, Buffalo,
New York, by The Steel Storage
and Elevator Construction Co.,
1897. (From *The Industrial Empire of
Niagara*, 1919)

Electric Elevator, shortly before
demolition. (Photo, Bazelon)

marine towers containing the legs, with the stiff one on the right, the loose one on the left. They were almost identical in form—plain rectangular boxes rising the full height of the house behind and capped by small double-pitched roofs of almost the same dimensions as the roof of the main building behind them. Since the exposed side wall of the stiff leg was flush with the end wall of the house, the side elevation presented a curious double-gabled silhouette, unlike anything else produced by elevator architecture in this period. Again we are confronted with an experimental and transitional building of unusual form, and with a design that has nothing tentative or unconvincing about it. Rather, a secure older vernacular of tall black sheds at the waterside, of which fragments remain all over northern Europe, was echoed here, and one must wonder whether this was a deliberate recall or just the "racial memory" of the trade.

The same confident-looking good order was not as apparent in the arrangement of the bins, which clustered behind and beside these works. Their pattern has become increasingly difficult to understand visually, partly because of piecemeal demolition of the bins and partly because the bins were not all the same size. One main set had larger bins than the other, while a cluster of yet smaller bins were tucked behind the house into an awkward corner created by the geometry of the site, whose boundaries do not run back at right angles to the river bank. All the bins were plain, squat, riveted boilerplate affairs with slightly domed tops, painted white from time to time to reduce heat gain from sunlight.

The overhead horizontal transfer conveyors, in their own black corrugated claddings, radiated at various angles from the house and were carried clear over the bins on thin steel frames. The return conveyors were in concrete trenches (abandoned and permanently flooded by the time I saw them) below grade level, since the bins stood directly on their foundation pads. In the middle of the Second World War (and therefore strictly outside the scope of this study), the storage capacity at the Electric was tripled by the addition of what looks to be an extensive system of closely packed cylindrical concrete bins. In fact, these are self-but-

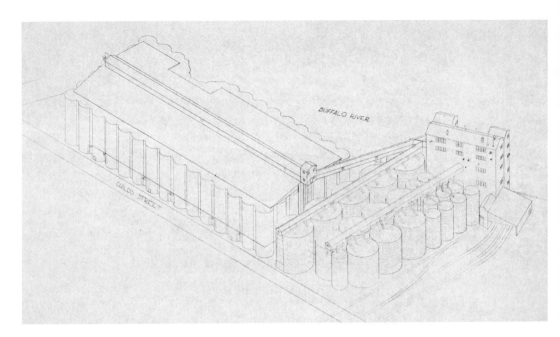

Electric Elevator. (Drawing by Matt
Johnston and Suzy Golczer)

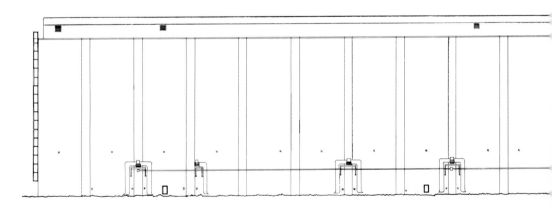

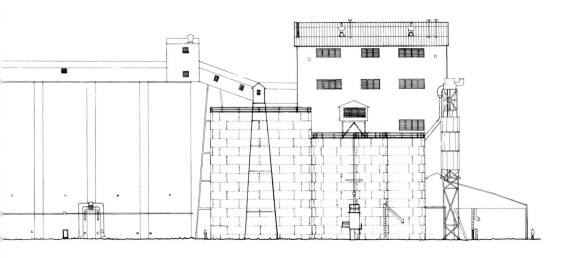

Electric Elevator. (Drawing by Matt Johnston and Suzy Golczer)

tressing concrete walls made of contiguous hollow-backed part-cylinders—half bins, in effect—used to enclose six enormous granaries that still stand and that are among the strangest monumental spaces I have ever entered. That the original legs and working house could accept this vastly multiplied operating load without visible alterations, let alone major extensions, is a tribute to the right conception of the original design.

That original conception and the mechanical innovations must guarantee the Electric an important place in the history of elevators, but its visual oddities and confusions were not likely to appeal to architects seeking to clarify their own style. Its only appearance in the European architectural literature reviewed for this study is among the set of aberrant illustrations to *Stil'i epokha* by the Russian constructivist Moisei Ginzburg. Even in the United States, however, it is rarely mentioned in literature of any sort, yet in introducing electric power, the loose leg, and the freestanding cylindrical bin, it effectively introduced the modern elevator.

What it did not introduce, probably because of the constricted site, was the equally modern practice of setting the naked bins in one, or possibly two, straight and parallel lines to make the most economical use of the Chase system. For the classic early demonstrations of that usage we need to turn back to Minneapolis, which, for the first decade of the present century, displaced Buffalo as the main center of innovation in the design of the parts of elevators devoted to storage. It was the next problem needing attention, and there was little to distract Minneapolitans from it. Their elevators made simple railcar-to-railcar transfers; because they were not located at the waterside in ports, they did not need the kind of leg invented by Joseph Dart for reaching deep into vessels, and the technologies for emptying railcars were already to hand. There may also have been some operational advantage in having elevators stand long and thin between the parallel tracks in the spreading railyards of the major *entrepôt* cities of the midwestern plains. This long format was eventually to become universal, even in terminal ports like Buffalo, but its definitive form first emerged in Minneapolis.

The Pioneer Steel elevator, which still proudly displays that name on its very tall working house, is among a select body of works that already showed the features of the type in 1901. It is also one of the very few of that epoch that survive—indeed the only one of the three great early boilerplate elevators mentioned above. As originally built, it must have been one of the most extreme examples of planning for the Chase system of horizontal, straight-line transfers, for its twelve main external bins stand in a single row continuing the line on either side of the house. Since they are eighty feet tall, they still dominate the scene, in spite of the fact that a secondary rank of lower tanks was added parallel to the first "almost immediately after these were completed."[3] Apart from the house—whose form, with its almost old-fashioned, tall, narrow clerestory, seems to echo the kind of wooden structures common in the previous century—the general shapes and the modes of connecting them are in the same idiom as at the Electric in Buffalo; but their vastly better state of preservation (the plant is still fully operational) adds to the contrast between the Pioneer's clear legibility and the Electric's apparent confusion. To see the Pioneer Steel elevator sitting, remarkably neat and clean, on a surface of pristine new snow, as was the case when I last saw it, is to get some idea of the impact that such structures must have had on those who were privileged to see them when they were new.

The two early steel elevators in Minneapolis are also missing from the European literature, which is surprising, since they do exhibit the clarity of form—"forms assembled in light" indeed—and the legibility of functional arrangements that the Europeans admired: "Their individuality is so unmistakable that the meaning of the structure becomes overwhelmingly clear to the passer-by."[4] However, there is a likely explanation for the absence of steel-framed structures of any sort whatsoever, let alone elevators with naked bins, from that literature of admiration. There was a decisive shift to concrete construction for elevators after 1900, not unlike the shift to concrete in factory building at the same epoch; and whether the Americans who supplied Gropius with his pictures were consciously of the concrete "party" or not, they may well have felt that an illustration of an elevator built out of anything else was too old-fashioned to be worth sending.

The switch to concrete, though decisive and fairly swift, was not uncomplicated. It took place against the expectations of the experts who wrote for construction industry magazines. An extensive and obviously well-researched article by John Kennedy of Montreal, which appeared in 1901, carefully reviewed all the advanced construction techniques for bins and silos—rectangular steel, cylindrical steel, cylindrical reinforced tile, and cylindrical reinforced concrete—and discussed and illustrated significant examples of each type. Kennedy then concluded that "steel would be altogether the most suitable and economical material."[5]

The probable basis for this honest mistake was that unlike steel, materials like tile and concrete were still conspicuously experimental, with barely a year of accumulated experience in bin-work compared to steel's longish prehistory. Most of that was outside the elevator business, admittedly, but it was still vastly more than existed in concrete anywhere at that time. Though the problems attendant upon the use of steel in bins and silos—rust, condensation, overheating, etc.— were well known by this date, there was probably no reason to suppose that differing but equivalent deficiencies might not be found in tile or concrete systems of construction.

However, a serious reason for concern about all cylindrical steel constructions was beginning to appear by the early 1900s, if one may judge from what is reported in the trade magazines of that epoch: they were less structurally stable when empty, or during emptying, than had been anticipated. In the late nineties and most of the first decade of the present century, *Engineering News* reported at least one structural collapse every twelve months, not of silos, but of a closely related structural type with dimensions comparable to those of a small bin: the cylindrical steel vessels known as "stand-pipes," which were used as header tanks and/or pressure-surge reliefs in public water-supply systems. Located on high ground, for obvious reasons, and therefore exposed to high wind-loadings, they seem to have been particularly prone to blow down when empty or, possibly, while emptying. The trouble seems to have been that unbraced cylinders of economically thin gauges of steel plate were less inherently rigid than had been supposed. In the right fall of light, for instance, one could see that at least two of the bins of the Electric Elevator had distorted slightly, or developed a kind of spiral wrinkling, and that the only thing preventing more extensive damage was the stiffening provided by the fairly substantial and slightly domed tops that covered them, something which the stand-pipes did not need and therefore generally did not have. Though covered bins benefited from this useful bracing, they were subject to a dangerous loading that could not affect open-topped stand-pipes: the vacuum effect that might occur if the grain were to let go suddenly during the emptying cycle. Since these dangers were already known, the need for a more inherently rigid form of construction for bins and stand-pipes alike must already have been in view.

But the means for more rigid construction was not available until the very end of the nineties, when Minneapolis produced two solutions. One, the tile bin, was to be short-lived but conceptually important; the other was the reinforced concrete bin, which was to become the "industry standard" worldwide. The primary motivation behind the invention of the tile bin, seems to have been achieving a more fireproof form of construction, since much of the technology and materials clearly came from the tile-built, steel-rod-reinforced floors and internal partitions increasingly used in big cities like Chicago at that time. Any other advantages that came with tile construction seem to have been side issues originally.

The dominant, and instantly successful, system for tile bins was the Barnett-Record (or Johnson-Record) System, for which the basic patents go back to 1895, although the system was not proven until 1899, when a single experimental tank was built, used, and evaluated in Minneapolis. The Johnson of the system's title was Ernest V. Johnson, son of the pioneer of fireproof elevator construction, George H. Johnson, whose eclectically constructed iron and brick Plympton elevator stood in Buffalo from 1869 until as late as 1902 (but seems to have been forgotten in that city). The Plympton, however, is as true an ancestor of the final tile system as was the elder Johnson of the younger, since it used cylindrical bins in very close array but naked and without any further exterior walling, the two-leaf cavity wall of special interlocking bricks being judged sufficient protection against the external climate.[6]

The basic technology of the system proven by the test bin built in 1899 was by modern standards a hybrid, consisting of a circular wall laid up of two leaves of special square tile. The inner and outer leaves were grouted together without a cavity, and the tensional loads were taken up by hoops of two-inch steel strap between the leaves. Although this system proved entirely satisfactory, to judge from observations made three years later,[7] it was substantially simplified in the improved version commonly employed thereafter. The latter used a single-leaf structural wall made of alternating courses of short and tall tiles; the short ones were hollow troughs into which the steel reinforcing rings were laid and then grouted down solid. Early versions of the simplified system apparently had a layer of glazed tiles lining the inner face of the wall to protect the grain or to prevent it from catching during discharge, but this was deemed unnecessary and these "furring" tiles were transferred to the outer face of the wall to protect the main structure against damage by external fire and weather. For a short period—barely a decade—the developed Johnson system must have been highly acceptable to the trade, for a very large number were built and still stand in their naturally handsome brown-to-purple, salt-glazed color range, a familiar part of the urban scenery of the elevator districts of cities from the Midwest up into Canada and across to the East Coast.[8]

In my own eyes, however, the strongest image of the tile elevator as an intermediary between the primitive phase of cylindrical bin construction and the classic concrete phase that was to ensue so soon after remains the St. Anthony 3 (now IMC) elevator at the Minneapolis end of the so-called

Electric Elevator, steel bins; concrete extension beyond by H. G. Onstad, 1940. (Photo, Bazelon)

IMC (St. Anthony 3) Elevator, Minneapolis, Minnesota, by The Barnett and Record Company, 1901. (Photo, Bazelon)

Midway elevator strip in St. Paul. Built in 1901 (and extended soon after), it was one of a group of Barnett-Record projects built in close order and widely noticed in the press at the time; but like Pioneer Steel it may now be the only survivor of its age and type. Two things are immediately and memorably noticeable about its appearance: one is its almost black color, which appears to be paint over the normal type of Johnson tiles; the other is its extreme simplicity of geometrical form. The house is a tall, thin rectangle with an almost flat roof and a skinny lean-to coming halfway up its side. The bins on the other side of the house are disposed in two parallel rows of eight each, and, as was the custom of their designer/builders, their forms are absolutely "pure" and basic, confused neither by contiguity with neighboring bins (there is always an air space between) nor by any "cupola" or horizontal-transfer housing over their heads, since the system, as originally used, ran the horizontal conveyors through the heads of the bins themselves.

What one sees are those "beautiful forms, the most beautiful forms" praised by Le Corbusier, pure and uncluttered but black against the green of the summer grass and scrub— or, more sensationally yet—black against white fresh-fallen snow in winter. Wilhelm Worringer's concept of the geometrical and abstract as the mark of the primitive in all arts and cultures—the source of Walter Gropius's belief that American engineers had retained some aboriginal *Sinn fur grosse, knapp, gebunden Form* (feeling for large, sparse, compact form) fresh and intact, and that their work was therefore comparable to that surviving from ancient Egypt[9]—all that European superstructure of aesthetics and cultural sensitivities begins to look like good sense when one sees these blunt abstract forms in high contrast against the equally abstract surface of the snow. If Worringer's later sneering reference to some "ultimate Metaphysic of Form"[10] to be found in North America has a metaphor of substance for me, it is in the sight of these grudging, lowering shapes crouched under a leaden winter sky, unlovable but compelling respect, the Protestant work ethic monumentalized.

Their color and their "Egyptian" forms also make them appropriately monumental in the funerary sense, for the death of the tile-bin system was at hand. The concrete system that doomed them was also Minneapolitan in its origins, and its development ran parallel in time, and, more extraordinary yet, in form and experimental method too. The first essay in concrete, an experimental, cylindrical, reinforced concrete bin known as Peavey's Folly, still stands in Minneapolis and now has National Landmark status—which, in view of its ultimate effect on industry nationwide and on modern architecture worldwide, it deserves more thoroughly than many other artifacts dignified with the same title. Cautious historians are inclined to describe it only as "probably" the first cylindrical concrete bin in the world,[11] but no rival has been discovered so far; and stories that once circulated to the effect that the Max Toltz of Great Northern Railroad fame had been building concrete elevators in Canada *before* 1900 are now known to derive from mistaken understanding of the evidence.

However, a fair amount of myth and mystification has always surrounded Peavey's Folly too, usually implying a European source for the system. In the basic form of the myth, its designers went to Europe in 1899 and, since they were known to have visited Berlin, were understood to have visited the Wayss und Freytag company to discuss the licensing of the Monier patents for reinforced cylindrical structures in concrete, which Wayss und Freytag had acquired some time earlier. Given the considerable hostility among many American entrepreneurs to the payment of licensing royalties of any sort (one recalls Henry Ford's long and successful battle to avoid the patent royalties levied on all automobile manufacture by George Selden), and since the designers were known to have inspected elevators in cities besides Berlin, it has been assumed that they might, alternatively, have been looking at rival systems that might help them circumvent the seemingly unavoidable Monier patents.

The truth, as established by extracts from the travel diary of Frank T. Heffelfinger of Minneapolis that were published in an article on the experimental bin by his daughter-in-law

Tile-bin construction system, George Johnson, 1869. (From *Reinforced Concrete Buildings*, 1912)

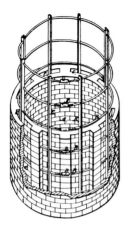

Johnson-Record trade plate, 1903.
(Photo, author)

Experimental concrete bin
("Peavey's Folly"), Minneapolis, Min-
nesota, by Frank H. Peavey and
C. F. Haglin, 1899. (Photo, Bazelon)

Ruth,[12] is less conspiratorial than the myths but sheds a revealing light on how enterprising, and international, life in "provincial" Minneapolis could be. The project to build an experimental bin in concrete was apparently discussed early in 1899 by Frank H. Peavey, already a large-scale international dealer in grain, and the local architect Charles F. Haglin. Construction of the single isolated bin was begun in the summer of the same year, using some type of climbing form-work that was raised as each section of concrete set, to form the shuttering for the next pour above. The walls were twelve inches thick at the base, and, as I understand it, reinforced by hoops of steel strap similar to those used on the experimental tile bin of the same year by Johnson and Record. It was 20 feet in diameter at the base and 68 feet high (thus comparable to the dimensions of the experimental tile bin) but was later raised to 125 feet, which is comparable to the largest concrete bins that later went into general service. The engineering work for all this appears to have been done by Haglin's office.

In the fall of that year, after the bin, already dubbed Peavey's Folly, had cured and was deemed safe, it was filled with grain and closed. This done, Haglin and Peavey's son-in-law Frank T. Heffelfinger left on their trip to Europe, with the intention of investigating prospects for trade in grain, especially with Russia, and of looking at the state of elevator construction in Europe as a way of monitoring their own work. The trip was no more than a moderate success; no deal was made in Russia, and although they saw a number of elevators in widely scattered areas of Europe and in a number of different proprietory systems, they saw no cylindrical bins made of concrete, were disappointed with the quality and performance of some of the concrete they did see, though much impressed with other bins, and apparently felt they had spoken with nobody who knew significantly more about the topic than they did.

Back in Minneapolis in the spring, Haglin supervised the discharge of the grain from the experimental bin in the presence of a fair-sized crowd, some of whom clearly expected the structure to implode when the grain began to flow. In fact, it did not, and the grain was reported to be in good condition after nearly six months in the bin. The new system was deemed a success, perhaps a little prematurely. In Duluth the Peavey Company's first full-sized elevator with cylindrical concrete bins—apparently begun before the successful demonstration of the experimental bin—suffered two widely reported collapses in the first three years of its life, the first in December 1900, before it was properly completed, and the other in May of 1903. The latter seems to have been due to settlement of the foundations and to the use of dirty aggregate,[13] but the first one suggests inexperience and faulty design.

The layout was an ambitious one, with fifteen bins in three parallel ranks, but the bins did not connect directly and thus brace one another. Instead there were short diaphragm walls, which, to simplify the shuttering, were presumably inserted only after the main cylinders had been cast. The walls created interstitials, spaces between bins that could be used for further storage volume, thus making more economical use of both the structure and the area of ground it covered. It was one of these interstitials that gave way while being filled with grain during preliminary testing and carried away the adjacent bin at the end of the rank. The collapse was presumably due to asymmetrical loading, though it is not clear if all, or any, of the adjacent main bins were filled; but it might not have happened, even so, had the structure been designed with the perimeters of the main bins, and their reinforcements, directly engaged with one another. The collapse was investigated by F. W. Cappelen on behalf of Lee Heidenreich, who, as manager of Monier patents in the United States, clearly had an interest in the good name of cylindrical concrete work; though it was C. A. P. Turner (who doubtless had an interest in the good name of engineering done in Minneapolis!) who wrote a letter to *Engineering News* explaining that

it is only fair to point out that the concrete and embedded steel construction used in the bins which failed is radically different from the Monier system which has been employed abroad and is being promoted in this country for elevator construction.[14]

Cappelen's report also implies that there was no vertical reinforcing in the bins that let go at Duluth, as there would have been in most versions of the Monier system, and one wonders if the Haglin-Peavey system might not have been too dependent on some other source of inspiration, such as the slightly earlier work on the Johnson-Record tile bins, with their simple, hooped reinforcement. Unfortunately, there is no mention of reinforcement of any sort whatever in Ruth Heffelfinger's narrative, though the detail in which she describes the operation of the traveling shuttering certainly gives the impression that it is some sort of eyewitness account. Nevertheless, Peavey's Folly did not collapse, and after its one test loading and emptying was put in honorable and conspicuous retirement and was never seriously used as a commercial elevator. It still stands, a slightly enigmatic shaft, isolated in a patch of grass next to a small factory devoted to trades that have nothing to do with the handling or processing of grain.

Whatever the mysteries surrounding it and the early days of the Haglin-Peavey system, the eight and half decades since its successful demonstration have invested it with a kind of mythic power, mostly in the eyes of the citizens of Minneapolis, for whom it is a source of civic pride, but also as the origin of a worldwide phenomenon. That larger connection is now part of the official myth in Minneapolis too; the landmark designation requires it, the literature confirms it, and the *Guide to the Industrial Archaeology of the Twin Cities,* with its specific reference to Le Corbusier, proclaims it.[15] All this is truly remarkable for a form of construction that, while undoubtedly revolutionary within its body of technology, had no ambition outside the realm of that technology and no ascertainable interest in creating symbols. Yet the cylindrical reinforced concrete bin rapidly became the prime constructive element in what might be termed the normative grain elevator and thus became a symbol of curious and ultimately atavistic power in America, as its characteristic silhouette came to dominate vast expanses of land, such as the prairies or the Texas Panhandle, where the only other object of enough bulk and height to compete with it for attention was the almost identical elevator in the next town. And outside the land of its birth, it was the form of these cylinders, assembled in light, that would provide the imaginations of European modernists with their most powerful icon of the Concrete Atlantis in the Motherland of Industry beyond the western ocean.

Adoptive Monuments of Modernism

The speed, momentum, and consequences of these rapid developments, from tile to concrete and then to increasingly sophisticated uses of concrete, are summed up and exhibited in the building history of the former Washburn-Crosby elevator complex (now General Mills) in Buffalo. It is also of the utmost importance to this study in a number of other guises: as an exemplary record of a swift historical process, as a surviving monument to the rise of the elevator in Buffalo, as a revelation to me of the possible richness and rewards of a study such as this, and as a continuing revelation to European modernists. In an earlier condition it was among the illustrations to Gropius's *Jahrbuch* article, and in a condition intermediate between that and the state in which I found it, the Washburn-Crosby was seen and photographed by an excited Erich Mendelsohn, suddenly confronted with the reality of his "silo dreams."

All this was not immediately clear to me; the complex has been endlessly modified to the point where it is unrecognizable from all viewpoints but one, and that is on the opposite side of the old Ship Canal, under the Skyway overpass on what seems to be part of the ground once occupied by the Dakota elevator (which Gropius also illustrated). Since the demolition of the Michigan Street lifting bridge, which is just discernible in one of Mendelsohn's photographs, there is little incentive to undertake the roundabout journey required to reach that particular piece of the riverbank, and my first inkling that I might be looking at something important came in the cockpit of a friend's boat as we went about in the Buffalo River. I soon confirmed that part of what I had seen also appeared in one of Mendelsohn's pictures in *Russland Amerika Europa,* but neither there nor in the earlier *Amerika:*

Bilderbuch eines Architekten is his captioning very helpful—the name of the elevator was not given, and in one case it was identified as being in Chicago![16] It seemed possible that one of the legs was also in Gropius's picture of the Washburn-Crosby, but to verify that I had to make that roundabout journey, then stand on some fairly dangerous and collapsible pieces of made-up ground (made up of garbage, in fact) in order to locate myself at what seemed to be the viewpoint of the *Jahrbuch* illustration, and then check the visible features of the current General Mills installation against a photocopy of the Washburn-Crosby illustration. There were enough correspondences to make the identification certain even before I tackled any other documents.[17] What those documents recorded of the transformations of the structure even before the *Jahrbuch* photograph was taken, and those that had been wrought upon it since, proved to be a capsule history of the industry and the building type.

The beginning was a set of nine Johnson-Record system tile bins, in the angle between the Ship Canal and the approach to the Michigan Street bridge. They date from 1903 and were attached to, and served, a straightforward, six-story, brick-pier milling building, almost inevitably designed by the Reidpath office. These are the bins at the extreme right of the Gropius picture, in which the mill behind them is

Washburn-Crosby (now General Mills) Elevator, Buffalo, New York, by Bateman and Johnson, and mill by R. J. Reidpath and Son, both 1903. (From *Buffalo Today*, 1906)

Washburn-Crosby, tile bins, present
state. (Photo, Bazelon)

hidden from the camera. Nowadays the bins themselves are hidden by a more recent mill built in two stages, one before the Mendelsohn illustration and one since. The bins are now boxed in by the newer building in front and the stub that remains of the old one behind, but they are easily visible from Michigan Street. Their original trade-plate tiles, giving the system's name, the dates of the patents, and the name of the proprietary company (Bateman and Johnson), survive, and each bin has one at about knee level, which is their usual location on all sets of Johnson bins known to me. Like most of the rest of this end of the complex, the bins have now been painted a light sandy color, so that their characteristic warm ceramic tones are not seen, though their different surface from all the concrete bins on the site can be discerned in every early illustration.

The next set of bins, in the center of the Gropius picture, seems to have been added before 1906 and the bins are already in concrete, which gives some idea of the speed with which the new material took over. The third set, on the left in Gropius and called Elevator C in some documents, is also in concrete and can be dated to 1909 by the building permits in City Hall. With these came the very imposing leg that appears in the *Jahrbuch* picture and the horizontal transfer that runs across the heads of all three sets of bins; in the end, that unique conveyor housing is the most recognizable

Washburn-Crosby, condition in 1909. (From *Jahrbuch des Deutschen Werkbundes,* 1913; courtesy Avery Library, Columbia University)

Washburn-Crosby, condition in
1918. (From *The Industrial Empire of
Niagara,* 1919)

feature in any picture of Washburn-Crosby in which it can be seen. The Gropius picture also shows no buildings of consequence behind the bins, but additional milling and shipping plants on that side must have been started shortly after. The rest of the bins on that side, visible in the Mendelsohn photographs, also began to appear very soon, first in a series of building campaigns that lasted until at least 1916 and then in another in the twenties.

In the earlier campaigns there were sensational advances in both construction technique and conceptual attitudes. The technique, barely a decade old at the beginning of this set of extensions, was so fully mastered that it could be literally turned inside out, as in the very conspicuous reversed curvature where the first new set of bins is attached to the last rank of bins of Elevator C. What had formerly been a strictly cylindrical form of construction of both limited and limiting capability became a far more flexible and adaptable instrument of spatial enclosure. Further evidence of this can be seen by examining the rest of this "facade." It does not consist simply of a series of ranked cylinders butting against each other, but of a series of segments, each of which is barely equal to a quarter-cylinder, that visually imply that the cylinders actually intersect one another. This, clearly, cannot be the case, and what one actually sees in every alternate quarter-cylinder is an "external interstitial," in plan a kind of curve-sided triangle inserted in the groove between one full cylinder and the next.

Washburn-Crosby was not the first elevator where such externals had been included, however; they had been attempted elsewhere in tile construction as well as concrete and had not always been successful. In Springfield, Ohio, an external interstitial on a concrete elevator had let go in 1910; the lower part burst outward and the falling grain caused a vacuum that sucked the upper part inward. Since the reinforcement of the interstitials was not tied back into that of the main bins, someone may have been trying to advance the technology faster than was reasonable. Properly tied and reinforced, of course, such external interstitials could greatly stiffen the outer rows of main bins, and it was probably only a matter of time before someone observed that such a succession of quarter-cylinders could form a strong, self-buttressing wall. The versions that were eventually built, as at the Electric Elevator extension in Buffalo, commonly employed much more than quarter-cylinders, in a properly cautious search for maximum stability.

Returning to the Washburn-Crosby, there is an even more remarkable and consequential development to be seen on that elevation of the complex: a second stiff leg. It may at first go unrecognized for what it is, since, unlike every other leg, loose or stiff, that survives in Buffalo, it is made by modifying the design of one of the regular bin cylinders. It is not an existing bin modified, but a specially built structure standing a little detached from the bins behind and noticeably taller. It differs from a regular bin in having windows in its sides, a different form of capping, and a long slot down the front to accommodate the raising and lowering of the bucket conveyor. Such deviations from normal bin design could not be accomplished after it had been built, at least not without unreasonable expense. So the structure must have been designed as we now see it; and we are left wondering what radical engineer, what genius of the *ad hoc,* conceived this transformation of a vessel invented for storage into a structure employed for the support of machinery and shelter for the men who served it? City Hall permits identify the contractors for this part of the complex as James Stewart and Co. of Chicago but do not name any engineer or architect. The only architect of title recorded for any part of the complex in this period of its development was A. E. Baxter of Buffalo, who was responsible in 1910 for the concrete-framed milling building that lies along the river bank in front of the first and second sets of bins. Baxter was to collaborate in the design of many later elevators, but his "architecty" contributions are easy to recognize by their preoccupations with style rather than function and their generally conservative, not radical, strain.

Washburn-Crosby, as photographed
by Erich Mendelsohn, 1924; milling
block added by A. E. Baxter, 1922.
(From *Amerika: Bilderbuch eines
Architetkten*, 1926)

General Mills (formerly Washburn-
Crosby) Elevators, present state.
(Photo, Bazelon)

General Mills, "stiff" and "loose"
marine legs. (Photo, Bazelon)

Whoever did that leg, the conceptual leap is striking; and the idea that the concrete cylinder might simply be a constructional device that could be used to support or contain matters other than grain was to be widely exploited. In many cases, for instance, the lowest part of the cylinders below grade level is used to accommodate the horizontal transfer conveyors, which was more economical than digging a separate trench below the foundations of the bins or raising the bins above ground on a separate concrete frame or table, as Baxter usually did in the elevators with which he was involved. But sometimes a whole cylinder within the regular pack of bins would be reserved for machinery, or offices and toilets would be inserted. All this, of course, has a curious effect on one of the persistent interests of the present study—the common notions of "functionalism." It is no longer so immediately clear to the passerby what the various parts of the structure mean, as Walter Gropius had supposed in 1913, since a cylinder might be a bin or a leg, might contain grain, machinery, or men. Functionalism, as commonly understood, has always seemed to suppose that every function has a corresponding optimum form that makes it recognizable, but at Washburn-Crosby and its progeny, engineers "not in pursuit of an architectural idea, but guided simply by the necessities of an imperative demand" (or so Le Corbusier claimed) were making nonsense of that treasured concept.

The rest of the history of Washburn-Crosby, as it affects this study, can be briefly given, since at the next point of chronological reference—Erich Mendelsohn's visit of 1924—the structure was in almost its present condition. Baxter's four-story milling block is clearly visible in the Mendelsohn photographs, but the third leg is not yet in place; it was a loose leg of a conventional steel-framed type and was added in the late twenties. The rest of the bins in the main cluster at the north end of the complex date from just after that period, as does the eight-story milling block squashed between Baxter's mill and the original tile bins on Michigan Street. The partial demolition of the original Reidpath mill of 1903 appears to have followed soon after.

The result of all this activity, as complex and as additive/subtractive as the work on a Gothic cathedral, is a structure that is conspicuously deficient in the kind of classical or functional "clarity" that appealed to a Gropius or a Le Corbusier, though its picturesque "dynamism" and appearance of "organic" growth could well have appealed to an expressionist like Mendelsohn or other modernists of a less puritanical persuasion. Most long-standing complexes that have survived changes of function, trading patterns, or productive technology will obviously present a similarly disorderly appearance to Gropius's hypothetical passerby, though they usually make perfectly good sense to those who manage and work in them. Yet it is remarkable how many elevators retain the visible logic of their original designs, even in Buffalo, with its frequently cramped sites and equally frequent changes in the nature of its trade. In some cases, this retention of the original image is simply due to sudden abandonment or failure to invest in new equipment and structures after the catastrophic collapse of Buffalo's once-central position in all North American movement of grain. In 1943, at its absolute peak, Buffalo was reckoned to be the largest and busiest grain port in the history of the world; by 1980 there was almost no movement of grain through the port except to serve local mills, and much of what survived did so only because of politically adjusted freight rates, as between waterborne and railborne carriage.

For historians, of course, these unaltered survivors are a great boon since they enable us to compare different solutions in organization, plan, section, construction, and (where it had survived local scrap dealers) machinery under almost "museum" conditions. One of the most instructive aspects has already been mentioned: the management of the spaces for the horizontal transfers underneath the bins. The bottom of a bin had to be fairly steeply sloped to prevent the grain from lodging, jamming, or bridging, and the logical way of achieving this under a circular bin was to make the bottom a deep, open, inverted cone, usually of steel boilerplate construction, with a valve to control the outflow of grain at the opening. Below the valve there was customarily a spout to direct the flow without spillage into the conveyor belt that effected the transfer; and the conveyor itself, complete with the chassis that carried it, added another eighteen inches to the depth of the whole array. All this often added up to an extra eight to ten feet below the bottom of the cylinder proper. More economical arrangements were possible by having flatter cones in the bin bottoms, omitting the spouts, and bringing the valve as close as possible to the conveyor; but this usually left only the most exiguous spaces through which service crews could stoop and crawl and made maintenance very difficult. There were good and necessary reasons for having a conveyor chamber of some height; the problem was how to provide it under a row of circular structures.

In what appears to have been a primitive phase in Buffalo, before interstitials were exploited and the bins still stood separately, an octagonal basement was built above ground level. These basements had doors and windows on their exposed faces, and the party wall between one octagon and the next was omitted to leave a clear passageway through the whole row of basements. That passage was wide enough for the conveyor but not usually men as well, though this was no great problem if each basement had access via a door from the outside. In most early examples known to me, however, such as the third phase of Washburn-Crosby or the former Canadian Government Elevator outside Calgary, Alberta (notable chiefly because it was illustrated by Le Corbusier in *Vers une Architecture*[18]) the octagonal basements are all buried below ground, and access to the conveyor spaces is difficult unless the machinery is shut down and the crew can climb along the stationary conveyor belt.

Putting the basements underground, then, is not necessarily progress, and it is interesting to see what happened when the Perrot elevator in Buffalo was extended in 1933. The old part had a classic set of raised octagons, and there were good (though not absolute) reasons for setting the new work on a base of the same height. This was in fact done, but the separate bases were coalesced into a single, long, rectangular chamber whose modernity was underscored by the insertion into its exposed wall of an equally singular, long, rectangular International Style window.

The author of this particular architectural contrivance was A. E. Baxter, who was extensively involved in the design of grain elevators and gave his preferred raised-basement treatment (though not always his decorative details) to a number of elevators in the Buffalo area. Thus, in the first phase of the Standard Elevator (1928) across the river from the Electric and in the gigantic Concrete Central Elevator (1915–17) further upstream, he sets the entire complex of bins one story up from wharf level on a kind of raised table, a continuous concrete slab carried on the legs of a concrete frame. This creates an exceptionally generous overhead height; and in Concrete Central in particular, one has a sensation of light and space to spare, since there are clear "aisles" between the windowed outer walls and the conveyor belts. These aisles are mostly twelve feet high and open out at one point to form an electrical switch room, which, with its control panels made of sheets of marble (for electrical insulation, not decorative ostentation), was palatial in size compared with what was customary in the trade.

Baxter's preferred solution was not generally accepted and became increasingly rare, probably because it was regarded as being too expensive for use except in unusual circumstances. Rather, the sophisticated bin-building techniques already mentioned offered the neatest and probably the most economical solution available in the classic period of elevator building. As represented in the Marine A elevator in Buffalo (1925), the solution was simply to put the bins on foundations some six feet below grade level and pierce their walls at the bottom to allow the conveyors to pass through. It was not all that simple to achieve, of course; the walls of the bins had to be thickened for the last ten feet to compensate for the support lost in the missing sections of wall (Marine A also has an added pilaster on the outside of each bin, apparently to provide extra material to pick up the supports of the conical steel bin bottoms). Special shuttering also had to be inserted to block out the openings during the pouring of the concrete: this shuttering could be reused, though not too easily if the site construction supervisor insisted on large parts of the work being finished up to the same level at the end of each day (which specifications often require) because this would lock up several sets of shuttering at once and prevent their being used *seriatim*. A fair amount of special reinforcing bar would also have to be bent up to fit around the openings, though this would be repetitive enough in practice for it not to be a serious diseconomy; Marine A, for instance, has 3 rows of bins with 12 main bins in each row plus interstitials, requiring therefore 117 openings between bin bottoms as well as 26 external doors—which adds up to plenty of work for the bar bender.

The resulting underground workspace, though less immediately attractive than in Baxter's designs, has a powerful character of its own, especially in the stripped and ruinous condition in which Marine A now finds itself. Conveyors, machinery, and sometimes complete steel bin bottoms have been removed since the plant was abandoned, creating sequences of empty, littered, circular "rooms" some twenty feet in diameter, connected by interstitial "lobbies" whose walls curve inward from the corners, more often than not— a very baroque effect. These spatial sequences are liable— like so much else about old elevators—to put one in mind of ancient Rome: the catacombs most obviously, though the spatial complexities here might stir echoes of Hadrian's villa or even the *Domus Aurea* of the emperor Nero. Fanciful this may be, yet how could the remains of these adoptive monuments of modernity touch our sensibilities if they nowhere connected to the ancient traditions of the "arts of well building"? The founders of modernism may well have been mistaken or self-deceiving in much of what they read into their photographic icons of the Concrete Atlantis, but the sense of rediscovering the ancient truths of some eternal architecture does seem proper in places like the catacombs of the Marine A Elevator.

Externally, Marine A exhibits those ambiguities of functional expression that have already been noted in connection with developed bin-construction technology. Its forms, as

Standard Elevator, Buffalo, New
York, first phase by A. E. Baxter,
1928, additions 1942. (Photo,
Bazelon)

Marine A Elevator, Buffalo, New
York, 1925. (Photo, Bazelon)

Marine A, bin bottoms. (Photo, Bazelon)

Marine A, cleared basement. (Photo, author)

such, are perfectly clear and uncluttered: a well-modulated wall of regular bins and interstitials, rising in almost unbroken verticality to their flat lids; extremely simplified, skeletal headworks served by the two loose legs on the wharf side; and a single tall house at one end. Nothing could be more pure and clear, nor more grateful to the classicizing European tastes of the twenties. But once again Gropius's observant passerby could be deceived about the meaning of the parts unless he paused long enough for some close reading of the details. The outside cylinder at the northeast corner has an external staircase (or its badly rusted remains, these days) zigzagging to a door high up in its side, and above that are large ventilating grilles, bespeaking the existence of machinery of some sort within. Once more the classic functional form of the grain container proves to contain, not grain, but something different. I have never been up to investigate its contents; that staircase was hardly an attractive proposition to one who bears permanent scars caused by other explorations of the same elevator!

Before leaving the Buffalo River and its elevators, it would be proper to review the other surviving works there, besides the Washburn-Crosby, that were demonstrably known to European modernists. Erich Mendelsohn shows a picture of the two legs of what is now the Peavey elevator and milling complex, which adjoins the Electric Elevator, and except that the legs have come to permanent rest a slightly different distance apart from that shown in the picture, the view of them from across the river is almost exactly as he recorded it. Mendelsohn and Moisei Ginzburg also show the unmistakable Kellogg elevators, whose unique form has a very instructive history. Originally there were two brick and wood elevators, Kellogg A and Kellogg B, on either side of a dock that had been dredged out of the bank of the Buffalo River. A milling building in the unmistakable brick-pier style of the Reidpath office was at the back of Kellogg A. Sufficient photographic evidence[19] survives to show what happened to this group of buildings after about 1915. First, Kellogg B was demolished and replaced by a regular set of what may be Baxter-designed bins, with a corrugated iron

Kellogg (now Schaeffer) Elevator, Buffalo, New York, as photographed by Erich Mendelsohn, 1924. (From *Amerika: Bilderbuch eines Architekten,* 1926)

Kellogg, condition in ca. 1917 before demolition of A elevator. (From *The Industrial Empire of Niagara,* 1919)

Kellogg, present state. (Photo,
Bazelon)

American (now Peavey) Elevator,
Buffalo, New York, as photographed
by Erich Mendelsohn, 1924. (From
Amerika: Bilderbuch eines Architekten,
1926)

Peavey Elevator, present state.
(Photo, Bazelon)

house and a characteristically shaped corrugated metal "cupola" on top of its headworks. From this cupola, a high-level horizontal transfer was projected across the dock to connect with whatever would eventually stand on the site of the recently demolished Kellogg A. Pending such building, the unconnected end of it was supported on a temporary steel lattice, which can be seen in photographs taken around 1920. Between then and the arrival of Mendelsohn in 1924, the entire complex (except the mill) on the A side was demolished and one bin built to accept the end of the horizontal transfer. That is the condition in which Mendelsohn found it, looking rather grotesque. But after that almost nothing happened except continued demolitions; and by the time I first saw it, there were still only a few more bins, some of them short ones, on that side, and all the rest was a desert of rubble.

That concludes the survivors still visible in Buffalo, with one striking exception that may properly be included in this roster although it did not figure until the very end of the twenties. In *Modern Architecture,* which the German modernist Bruno Taut published in both English and German in 1929, not only are a number of grand old Functionalist classics like the Crystal Palace prominently featured to support his arguments, but also the Canadian Government elevators in Montreal, in a different view from that in Gropius and Le Corbusier, and Concrete Central in Buffalo. The latter thus has the distinction of appearing for the first time in what seems to be a book—possibly the first book—specifically intended to introduce modern architecture to a well-informed, art-loving, English-speaking audience. However Taut came to choose Concrete Central, it provided a fitting conclusion to what had been a stirring period of elevator building in the United States and of elevator rhetoric in Europe. Like the spectacular photograph of the Ford River Rouge plant by Charles Sheeler, which appears unacknowledged in European publications like Moholy-Nagy's *Von Materiel zu Architektur,*[20] the appearance of Concrete Central in *Modern Architecture* may be seen as the last fine flourish of the first explorations of the Concrete Atlantis.

Unlike the River Rouge plant, however, whose vast single-story worksheds represented a critical break from the now almost defunct tradition of the concrete-framed Daylight factory that the Europeans were to admire long after its demise in America, Concrete Central shows us the grain elevator, the other half of that body of European admirations, still flourishing at the end of the twenties, as it would continue to do for almost another two decades.

Taut's illustration shows it flat on, squatting enigmatically low on the far side of an almost equally enigmatic flat landscape in which, nevertheless, a specially dredged and straightened reach of the Buffalo River lies just hidden from view. Although it is still possible, at some risk to life and limb, by climbing across railroad bridges and the like, to see Concrete Central from the other side, that is the less interesting and less familiar side of the complex, offering nothing to the view but hundreds of bins and interstitials. The more familiar and more rewarding view is the one shown in Taut of its wharf side and its three loose legs, though now it must be seen over a jungle of undergrowth that lies between the river and the lower reaches of Katharine Street. Closer views are not normally to be had, unless one goes up river to it by boat or is prepared to undertake an adventurous and circuitous safari on foot—it is completely inaccessible by wheeled vehicles these days—through thickets of red sumac bushes and along rusting rail tracks.

That journey is worth it, however. In lonely but not yet totally ruinous abandonment, this huge rippled cliff of concrete dominates a quarter-mile reach of the river. It is truly enormous in scale; its capacity of four and a half million bushels made it the largest elevator in Buffalo and one of the largest ever built anywhere. For comparison, it is about twice the bulk of recent megastructures such as Cumbernauld Town Center or Centre Pompidou, but because it consists almost entirely of closed storage volumes to which there is no casual access, it remains impermeable, secret, and aloof. There are some elevators where one can penetrate into gigantic storage volumes—the Electric extensions of 1940, for instance—and marvel at their sheer dimensions, but at Concrete Central the storage volumes remain as inaccessible as the interior of an Egyptian pyramid, to use an exotic comparison whose propriety may emerge in the last section of this book.

The first time I reached Concrete Central by land, a series of incidents emphasized its abandonment and isolation. Shrubbery had already begun to grow out of its upper works, inviting a comparison with Roman ruins that was enhanced by the flight of a bird of prey from the head-house at the sound of my approach. That sound was amplified when my foot crashed through a rotted plywood cover that had been laid over an open culvert. As I extricated myself, I reflected on my folly: had I sustained an incapacitating injury, rather than mere scratches, in that fall, even those who knew approximately where I was would have no idea how to reach me, after they had finally decided they had waited too long for my return. I remembered the fate of the Chicago architectural photographer Richard Nickel, lying dead in the ruins of the Schiller theater for weeks before his body was discovered.

Yet the sense of distance from help and civilization was exhilarating rather than depressing; the presence of the huge abandoned structure produced a mood more elegiac than otherwise. Coming out on to the wharf, dominated by the three largest loose legs ever built in Buffalo, now semi-transparent as the winds of the winters had blown away more and more of their rusted corrugated cladding, it was difficult not to see everything through eighteenth-century picturesque visions of ancient sites or even Piranesi's views of the temples of Paestum. Longer study, however, suggested something more like the view that early Christian pilgrims might have taken of Rome: a double vision of something that was in itself ancient and therefore to be revered but that was also to be respected for a newer body of meanings laid over it by the beliefs of later peoples. I was looking at one of the great remains of a high and mighty period of constructive art in North America, a historical monument in its own inalienable right. But at a slight cultural remove, I was also—inevitably, given my European and modernist education

Concrete Central Elevator, Buffalo,
New York, by A. E. Baxter, 1915,
extended 1917–19. (Photo, Bazelon)

Concrete Central, head-house and
marine legs, present condition.
(Photo, Bazelon)

The Grain Elevator

in architecture—looking at a monument to a different civilization that had been as unknown to its builders as Christianity had been to the builders of most of the monuments in Rome: the culture of the European modern movement. As legendary symbols whose physical substance was unknown, the images of these great hulks had been co-opted to serve as exemplary structures by an almost alien culture.

We are, perhaps, too prone to treat modernism as if it were the same thing everywhere; in anthropologists' and sociologists' value systems, modernization seems to be almost synonymous with urbanization and to be seen as an homogenizing force—which is not unfair since one of modernism's most urban and energetic promoters, Le Corbusier, explicitly wished for an architecture that would be the same everywhere, "at the tropics and at the Poles." Yet in the presence of the great elevators of Minneapolis or Buffalo, I was struck again by the cultural width of the Atlantic, by the sheer gulf of space and missed understandings that separates these structures, admirable and remarkable as they are in purely American terms, from those who had never stood as close to them as I did and who admired their images under quite other lights. The difference between the tangible fact and the utopian vision of a Concrete Atlantis seemed perfectly clear to me, but I wondered if it had also struck informed visitors like, say, Erich Mendelsohn. Did he never sense another reality behind these manifestations of his "silo dreams"? Was the vision double for him, as it was for me, or did he see it with the single eye of faith, in the heyday of that idea of modernism, now in decline, that we have wished upon these our adoptive ancient monuments?

Afterthoughts: Survival and Obsolescence

The survival of so many important and influential monuments of the early period of modern industry in cities like Buffalo must obviously give architectural historians great satisfaction, but it should also give them pause and make them ask why and how this gratifying situation has come about. The first part of the answer is chilling: the world at large, and the world of industry in particular, does not share the architectural historians' belief that there is some moral or cultural obligation to conserve such structures; with the exception of Peavey's Folly and Ransome's bridges in Golden Gate Park, none of the buildings or installations discussed in this study have been acknowledged by landmark designation *for their architectural significance* or preserved out of any sense of cultural obligation. Minneapolis clearly values Peavey's Folly, and its landmark designation came about largely through local initiative. The city of San Francisco seems to have no discernible interest in Ransome's work, in spite of the enormous long-term consequences of his activities there. And the city of Buffalo has only very recently begun to show the slightest interest in its surviving elevators, and still seems to have none at all in the remains of the Larkin company's plant.

The last matter should direct attention to the curious ways in which cultural values are incorporated into everyday politics, and there handled. Buffalo has suffered such execration because Frank Lloyd Wright's Larkin *A* building was allowed to be destroyed that the city seems to have assumed that the remainder of the plant had no comparable historical value. In this it has been the victim of the inattention and ignorance of the general body of architectural culture; to denounce the demolishers of a Wright building without having visited it in the flesh, without knowing whether or not it was a *good* building by the master, seems to me irresponsible. As far as now can be ascertained, and in spite of a longish list of well-remembered shortcomings, it seems that Larkin *A* was indeed a remarkably good building, but the execration is entirely over the demolition of any building whatsoever that bears Wright's name. As usual, the cognoscenti have chosen to believe the name on the label, not the quality of the specific product, and the reputations of the unlabeled buildings all around have suffered in consequence—as is evidenced by the fact that the good people at Graphic Controls Incorporated, to whom we are all indebted for the sound state of the Larkin R/S/T building, were originally under the impression that it was a Wright design! Nor were they alone in this; when the Aberthaw Construction Company's album of progress photographs of the erection of

R/S/T resurfaced, it was offered for sale as being a record of the construction of the Administration building, since no other major structure for the company was known.

Observers of the Buffalo scene who were sensitive to good architecture, rather than simply responsive to famous names, would surely have been forced to acknowledge that a number of structures of unusually high quality stood around the Administration building while it survived, and still stood around its cleared site after it had gone. But even Erich Mendelsohn, who visited the Administration building in the morning before his exciting visit to the grain elevators, seems to have nothing to say about the rest of the plant. Perhaps to his modernist eyes the other buildings were just "old-fashioned factories," though even he could have never have said that about R/S/T had he actually seen it. Of course, it is possible that his guides to Buffalo were "of the party of Mr. Wright" and had no interest in showing him anything else.

Even so, it is remarkable that Henry-Russell Hitchcock, at a time when he was most likely to be of the Wright party, seems to have been the only writer or historian to mention any of the other Larkin buildings in the same text (if not the same paragraph) as the A; just as remarkable, alas, has been the continuing rarity of mentions until very recent times. Even now appreciation of such structures rarely becomes apparent until the last occupying enterprise closes down or until they are threatened with demolition. In the common run of local politics, it is only as they lapse into picturesque decay that they are found admirable, become the focus of battles over zoning or urban renewal, are admitted to the canons of industrial archaeology and, with luck, are sometimes deemed worthy of elevation to the status of Historic Landmarks or National Parks.

It is not my intention here to satirize either industrial archaeology or the National Parks Service, both of which I generally hold in high esteem, but the combined effect on the public has been to leave the kind of building discussed in this study still far beyond the grasp of our general culture. Well-presented places like Coalbrookdale in Britain or Troy,

New York, in the United States so dominate the public view of industrial history that sites and buildings that do not conform to that imagery ("the industrial-archaeological style of architecture," I have heard it called) continue to be overlooked. Lowell, Massachusetts, seems to me curiously deceiving, almost, in these matters; what was of crucial importance about Lowell was far less its mill buildings, which look rather sad in their present antiseptic isolation, than the extraordinary paternalistic industrial culture that flourished in and around them and made the town a byword for good management and good social order. Yet the surviving structures around the visitor orientation center maintained by the Parks Service can tell us nothing about the benevolently regimented daily lives of the famous Lowell mill girls. And in terms of the social history they are now supposed to monumentalize, the preservation of the mills is only marginally more relevant than the preservation of Shakespeare's alleged birthplace is to literature, and considerably less so than the preservation of Thomas Jefferson's Monticello is to practically everything about the history of the United States.

The elevators, mills, and factories of Buffalo, Minneapolis, Detroit, or even Rockville, are important in themselves, as monuments to the history of the building arts or to the technical innovations—as at Ford's New Shop—that made the invention of new building types necessary. But there is no way—except allusively and most obliquely—that any building at any of the Ford plants could monumentalize Ford's most consequential social innovation, the five-dollar-a-day wage, and only an ill-informed belief in the imagined "seamlessness" of the web of modern culture or in the "totalizing" tyranny of capitalist ideology could make anyone suppose otherwise.

There are better ways to remember social innovations than in preserving the buildings, constructed for a previous regime or social order in which they just happened to take place; and there are more convincing reasons for preserving historic factories and mills—because they are important to the history of building, for instance, or because they are better architecture than the common expectations of their

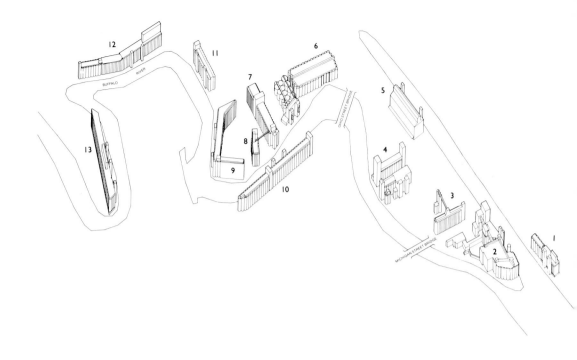

172

Grain elevators of the Buffalo River District. (Drawn by Cherie Wendelken and Bud Jacobs)
1. Connecting and Terminal
2. General Mills
3. Kellogg
4. Agway
5. Pillsbury
6. Cargill Electric
7. American
8. Perot
9. Lake and Rail
10. Standard
11. Marine A
12. Cargill Superior
13. Concrete Central

The "Midway" Minneapolis–St. Paul, Minnesota. (Photo, Bazelon)

times required. Here again, however, some confusing considerations must be acknowledged. Buildings can be important to architectural history for reasons that have nothing to do with those for which they were originally built.

It could be argued, and with very little exaggeration, that Elevators *A, B,* and *C* of the Washburn-Crosby complex constitute the most internationally influential structures ever put up in North America because of their effect on the architectural vocabulary of the generation of the founders of modern architecture. It is not an argument that cuts much ice in Buffalo, or not yet, partly because the complex is not in itself of outstanding or inherent importance to the history of the city or its trade, in the way that Joseph Dart's original elevator might be if it still stood. The contrast here with Minneapolis is instructive; quite apart from the almost unbelievably different economic fortunes and civic styles of the two cities, Minneapolis does have a standing monument—Peavey's Folly—that not only focuses the local historical interest, but is now also perceived as being of international importance as well, as the very first of the "first fruits of the New Age."

At Peavey's Folly, the extrinsic importance that has accrued to a structure originally built without any conspicuous cultural or international aspirations can comfortably be recognized and is seen as reinforcing its purely American or local claims to public attention. Buffalo, at the time that I began work on this study, did still possess a large (though constantly wasting) part of an industrial monument of equal historical importance, and one that abundantly deserved that kind of reinforcement: the Electric Elevator. For all its strong claims to international primacy—the first built specifically to use steel bins, the first with electrical power, the first with a loose leg—it had fallen on very hard times, long since abandoned as a working elevator and with all the lineaments of a structure doomed to creeping demolition, like an old Roman fortification being picked apart for its bricks by some Teutonic tribe that knew nothing of architecture. By the time this chapter was completed, all the steel parts had been torched and removed, leaving a wide hole in what had become for me a familiar riverside scene. The reason for this piecemeal demolition, I suspect, may have been a low-budget attempt to disencumber the site of everything that could hinder free and profitable access to the concrete extension added in 1940.

The concrete extension to the Electric is a visually deceptive structure, since what appear to be the conventional ranks of cylindrical bins are, in fact, the exterior convexities of self-buttressing walls made of ranges of contiguous three-quarter cylinders, with their open quarters facing into the six gigantic clear-span storage halls within. Even the partitions between these vast volumes are made of ranks of cylinders and part-cylinders of concrete, not used to contain grain, but to house machinery and equipment to power the winches that dragged man-guided scoops across the floor to move the grain about. Given modern rubber-tired front-loaders to move the contents around, and hall-to-hall openings large enough to allow the front-loaders to pass, this could be made into a bargain of a bulk-storage facility.

But this would reveal its true historical importance as well, as the prototype, as far as I can tell, of all other last-generation grain-storage facilities, which are simply very large, clear-span hangars with horizontal transfers under their floors and front-loaders moving around upon those floors. Versions of this ultimate machine-age granary are to be seen in nearly all the major *entrepôt* ports of North America; they are the type that has finally rendered the classic—dare one say "Corbusian"—elevator with its ranked cylinders obsolescent. One can hardly call that type terminally obsolete as yet because hundreds are still in use all over the world, and I have seen a cylindrical bin of the historic type being built by more-or-less the historic procedures in Montreal as recently as 1979! But they are now as effectively doomed as the classic Daylight factory was in 1917.

The concrete cylinder elevator is still so omnipresent because it represented an almost excessively good investment when first built. If it was solidly enough made to carry its load, maintain an equable thermal environment, and resist fire for long enough to amortize the original investment, then it had to be well enough made to last more or less

Electric Elevator, Buffalo, New York; surviving concrete extension after demolition of steel structures, 1984. (Photo, Bazelon)

forever—and be well enough made to be extremely costly to demolish. The impoverished community in Buffalo has not had the resources to demolish its concrete heritage, even when long since abandoned, and the only elevator of any consequence to this study (other than the Electric) to be totally removed is the steel-built Dakota, whose site was cleared to accommodate the underpinnings of the Skyway. Elsewhere there have been a few demolitions or attempted conversions, such as the creation of the Quaker Square complex in Akron, Ohio, out of the abandoned Quaker Oats plant and elevator and Ricardo Bofil's made-over cement silos in Barcelona, though most of the bins there seem to survive chiefly as a picturesque backdrop to more rationally reusable spaces. In general, however, the concrete grain elevator has been a conspicuously durable building type, resistant even to even skilled demolitionists, long after its physical functions and economic justifications have disappeared.

In such spectacular urban scenes as the view down the Buffalo River toward the Ohio Street bridge or that looking eastward through the surviving cluster of giant elevators on the Minneapolis Midway, one can see that the combination of assured durability and long-sustained functional relevance has

Electric Elevator extension, interior
bin and structure. (Photo, Bazelon)

given concrete elevators a monumental longevity far beyond that which technical progress has allowed their concrete contemporaries, the Daylight factories. Another factor complicating the survival of such factories, besides their having been replaced by the single-story workshed, is their location within the topographies of cities. The elevators were usually located near watersides or railyards, and the shifting patterns of transportation that have caused the decline of water and rail have excused those areas from competitive pressure to clear the ground for redevelopment. Such areas are rarely seen as desirable territory for new building; even the elevators in Minneapolis seem to have been stranded by a retreating tide of railborne commerce on vast expanses of land that interest nobody but the real-estate departments of the railroad companies. They have been left in comparative peace, unthreatened by demolition, as have elevator districts almost everywhere. So the removal of an elevator like the Dakota in Buffalo was a cause for comment, and the fact that it was removed to make way for a highway is a clue to the different fates suffered by factories and elevators.

During the 1950s and 1960s in particular, nothing was allowed to stand in the way of highway building, as urban historians and others have often lamented. These highway-building campaigns hit factory districts particularly hard. Whatever their transportation needs, factories had commonly been built closer to the downtown cores of cities than had elevators, and in their decline the territory the factories occupied was often handily placed to accept traffic improvements. As Procter and Matuzaski observed in *Gritty Cities*:

The old under-utilized mill buildings often provided the path of least resistance for freeways through cities. Both Waterford and Bridgeport saw major old industrial areas cleared out for new interstate highways to facilitate travel and commerce.[21]

It was not only Waterford and Bridgeport that underwent these clearances; with notable exceptions like Paterson, New Jersey, where energetic citizen action as much as anything else seems to have saved older downtown industrial areas from the intrusions by highways, this has been the common lot of the inner-ring areas surrounding downtowns in the crowded cities of the northeast. "Scenic," or, if you prefer, "catastrophic" clearances in Lowell or in Providence, Rhode Island, have seen downtown tidying up allied with traffic engineering to remove complete industrial topographies, and the whole thrust of urban renewal has been to remove such areas and their monuments. The survival of the Larkin complex in Buffalo has been at the expense, one might say, of other industrial zones nearer the center of the city, which have been cleared for highways and their feeder roads; while the dispersal of others, like the Pierce Arrow plant, by the creation of new, outer-suburban industrial sites along the Belt Line railroad, placed a substantial segment of Buffalo's Daylight factories outside the territory that traffic improvements were to overrun.

The other factors that militated against the long survival of the earlier multi-story factories were, of course, their early obsolescence as a building type and their replacement by single-story structures as the preferred containers for manufacturing processes. The story tells itself dramatically in Detroit, where the high-density Packard plant, with railyards alongside, is superseded by the linear Old Shop at Highland Park, with the railyards sandwiched between it and the machine shops. That was in turn superseded by the New Shop, through which the rail tracks actually pass, and then by the long, single-story sheds of the River Rouge, scattered over a remote suburban "green field" site far from any other industries or human settlements, and where connectivity by rail and road seems to dominate all other design considerations. And all this happened so fast that Charles Sheeler's famous Precisionist photograph of the industrial scenery of the Rouge appeared in Moholy-Nagy's *Bauhausbuch* in 1929, only six years after Le Corbusier's encomium of the multi-story type had appeared in book form in *Vers une Architecture*.

This drive toward the single-story workshed was not just a Ford mania; the type had a pre-history. From about the middle of the First World War, when the need to rapidly build factories for manufacturing munitions became paramount, single-story worksheds were established as the new norm for factories. They took form not only in the heroic constructions of Albert Kahn, but also through the more or less off-the-peg kits of parts supplied by the Austin Company in Cleveland, Ohio, and by others as the twenties proceeded. Despite the persistence of brick-pier construction on suitable, that is cramped, sites in New England almost to the time of the Great Depression, the multi-story daylit factory, of whatever material, was already doomed by the time the Buffalo Meter Company built what was to become Bethune Hall; and it was beginning to fade into the industrial sunset by the time Le Corbusier held it up for public admiration in the pages of *L'Esprit Nouveau*. A "great epoch" may have been coming for him, but one was just about over for the buildings that had inspired and confirmed his vision of the framed parts of a new architecture—which was really the true old architecture of the great tradition for him. As it ended, the classic epoch of the concrete-framed Daylight factory abandoned its monuments in a limbo where they were prey to demolishers and developers.

Prey also, one might say, to European architectural propagandists with axes to grind, and even to monomaniacal European industrialists with visions of "an American factory." In the words of Amedée Ozenfant, Le Corbusier's partner in art politics and co-editor of *L'Esprit Nouveau:* "Those who profess to love machinery usually prove to be collectors of antiques!"[22] European lovers of industrial architecture were also to prove to be antiquarians—not only the modernist architects, but even the boss of the Fiat automobile company, Giovanni Agnelli, who, possessed by American visions and mass-production ambitions, commissioned in 1916 a copy of Ford's Old Shop at Highland Park! The real America of "colossal utilitarian architecture of great form," as Wilhelm Worringer had said of the elevators, might indeed be an "area of civilization without myths," but Europe seems to have been the motherland of modern mythology.

What you regard as the ultimate metaphysic of Form is merely
the Americanism which otherwise you so much despise.

Wilheim Worringer, Egyptian Art

3

Modernism and Americanism

The Fagus Factory

At first sight it might well appear that the most appropriate place to begin an examination of the influence of all these exotic American industrial structures on modern European architecture would be the Faguswerke at Alfeld-an-der-Leine in northwest Germany. Generally regarded as one of the crucial founding monuments of European modernism, it was commissioned by entrepreneurs who admired America, sought American technical aid in modernizing their plant, and thereby secured American financing for its construction. Its architect of title not only described it as "an American shoe-last factory," but also published the article and illustrations that effectively introduced American industrial buildings to the European architectural profession and public.

The Fagus plant is indeed a highly appropriate place, but its relationship to America is not as simple as might immediately appear: confronting the building, one can sense something like American intentions or ambitions, but nothing substantive on which to hang the kind of art-historical comparisons from which influence is usually deduced. The building, as it stands, is as European as a Gothic cathedral. Nevertheless, these seeming contradictions can do much to help us enter "the mind of the times" and do nothing to detract from the quality of the design.

Faguswerk, Alfeld-an-der-Leine,
Germany, by Edouard Werner, succeeded by Walter Gropius and
Adolf Meyer, 1911–14; sawmill,
warehouse, and drying kilns. (From
Bauten der Arbeit und des Werkehrs,
1929)

Faguswerk, offices and boiler house.
(From *Bauten der Arbeit und des
Werkehrs*, 1929)

Faguswerk, plan of first phase, 1912.
(From *Bauten der Arbeit und des
Werkehrs*, 1929)

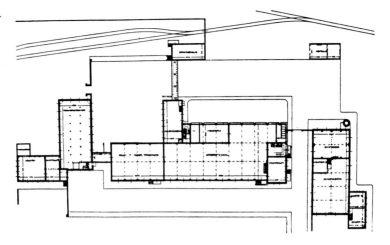

Soundly made in the beginning, and well maintained for
most of the time since, the plant has survived the biblical
three-score years and ten in excellent condition, though it is
now beginning to show its age. The "glass walls" that made
it so important a model of modernity have begun to bulge
out of plane in places, and diagonal cracks that traverse the
yellow brickwork bespeak structural settlement over the
years. Otherwise, all is much as it appears in the familiar
photographs that have illustrated every major book about
the modern movement. At least that is true of the more
public and commonly published sides of the works; around
the back one begins to see, alas, its most striking resemblance to the American factories that may be supposed to
have inspired it: the cobwebs and deathly pallor that abandonment and disuse bring to even the best maintained
industrial buildings, for only parts of the plant are now in
regular use.

One notices these signs of industrial mortality around the
boiler house in particular. The brick steps that lead down to
the basement and up to the main doors of the boiler house
itself have that unmistakable air of not being trodden upon,
though no grass had yet sprouted in their cracks when I saw
them in 1984. I also noticed—or, rather was reminded of—
something else about those steps. They are guarded by
proper industrial or "modern" handrails of standard steel

piping, with appropriate connections and bases—except that their ends, beyond the last upright at the newels, are wrapped around in fulsome Art Nouveau, or even Victorian, spirals.

At moments like this—and there are quite a few of them—Fagus is apt to appear far less "modern" than its committed apologists have supposed. One must say "supposed" because it can be shown, even on the internal evidence of their writings, that hardly any of those propagandists of the International Style had seen the building other than in photographs. The Italian historian Leonardo Benevolo, however, clearly had seen the plant with his own eyes, because he describes its site as only an eyewitness could have done. He too observes that it is not conventionally "modern" but looks back in many parts to the immediate pre-modern past:

The choice of details, particularly in the famous glass building, reveals numerous uncertainties: the ideal of making the glass protrude from the wall, the continuous glass at the corners, the main doorway, and the block of the building in which it is set, lined with darker horizontal bands of brick, are plainly references to Behrens' style, made with a certain amount of embarrassment. . . .

In this building an extremely fleeting moment of transition is crystallized, and this may be the explanation of its particular attraction.[1]

Though I cannot agree with the whole of Benevolo's lengthy interpretation of the building, his phrase "a fleeting moment of transition" is extremely well taken. This, however, does not mean that the design can be separated into elements that are more modern and less modern. Like that other masterpiece of transition, the School of Art in Glasgow by Charles Rennie Mackintosh, it seems all of a piece, occupying its uniquely intermediate position in the history of architecture with all the assurance of a fully realized work—which is all the more remarkable when one considers its convoluted building history and multiplicity of architects.

That history has still made little impression upon the established mythology of modern architecture, in spite of the fact that it was fully published by Helmut Weber as long ago as 1961[2] and was known to the movement's gossips long before that. Its complications need to be laid out here to a modest extent, however, because they illuminate some of the more intriguing aspects of the building and its peculiar relationship to the history of modern architecture as generally understood. The clients, Carl and Karl Benscheidt (father and son), had been the effective management team of an older company that still survives in Alfeld, but in 1910 Carl decided to move out on his own. He purchased a clear "green field" site by the railroad tracks on the northern outskirts of the town and hired Eduard Werner, a trusted local architect from Hannover with extensive industrial experience, to design his new plant.

He also opened negotiations with The United Shoe Machinery Corporation in Beverly, Massachusetts, for acquiring up-to-date manufacturing equipment, and, toward the end of the year, he went to the States to conduct the business with them personally. The result of this face-to-face encounter was that the corporation decided that Benscheidt would be an excellent partner in its attempt to establish footholds in the European market. It proposed a joint venture, to which United Shoe Machinery would contribute some Dm800,000 in capital, to be called *Fagus GmbH Alfeld* in honor of *Fagus Grandifolia,* the common beech tree whose wood was the raw material for the new company's main product—shoe lasts, the foot-shaped wooden form over which the parts of a shoe are shaped and joined.

This, surely, should be the first place to look for American influence on European factory design, but it is hard to find. There is no visible connection between that ultimate masterpiece of Ransome's declining years at Beverly and any of the versions of the design for what was to become the first masterpiece of Gropius's budding career. Indeed, the contrasts could hardly be more striking between United Shoe Machinery, a concrete-framed structure of strict and minimalistic rationality except for a few limited architectural grace notes of distantly classical extraction, and Fagus with its projected glazing and tapered-back brick columns. By American standards of early 1914, when Fagus was effectively completed, it was a rather old-fashioned brick-pier construction—albeit the design had been filtered by then through the talents of two, perhaps three, school-trained and sophisticated European architects who had contributed any number of design concepts, from the larger plan to the smallest of details, that were right outside the workings of the American industrial tradition.

It is possible, however, that the real effect of Benscheidt's American connection upon the final design was in the decision to employ Gropius as the architect. Hungry for work at that stage in his career, Gropius was in the habit of writing to every entrepreneur he knew (from following the trade journals, etc.) to be considering the erection of a building. His initial letter of December 10, 1910, to Carl Benscheidt (who was still in the United States) appears to be one of the very few that produced any effect. The credentials he gave to Benscheidt in offering his services were his experience in working on factory projects for the Allgemeine Elektrizitäts Gesellschaft while in the office of Peter Behrens and the name of a brother-in-law in Alfeld, Landrat Max Burchard, as a character witness.

In all honesty, one must wonder if—even given the great reputation of the Behrens office—these would have been enough to make Benscheidt transfer the design of the new plant to this unknown architect without some good external cause. He already had an architect on whom he could rely, and he probably already had a design, at least in sketch form, since the finished Werner design, with which he cautiously proceeded even while negotiating with Gropius, was approved by the local Baupolizei as early as April 28, 1911. The negotiations with Gropius also reveal that he was determined to retain what he regarded as the best and essential elements of Werner's project, for the freedom of action allowed to the younger architect was constrained, to put it mildly.

Throughout, Benscheidt underlined his commitment to Werner's wide experience in the field for the *innere Anordnung and Ausgestaltung* (internal layout and detailed design) of the scheme, because he did not believe he could do better; but in his reply of January 12, 1911, to Gropius's original letter, he said that he had decided otherwise about the *äussere Gestaltung* (external design) of the buildings. If Gropius was prepared to collaborate with Werner on this basis, he would be willing to use his services. This division of labor is emphasized in later letters: "Please examine these plans to see what you can do with the facade" (March 20); and again, "You will undertake the *architektonisch, künstlerische* [architectural, artistic] design of our factory, for which the main elements have already been designed by architect Werner . . . in order to give the whole plant a *geschmacksvoll* [tasteful, even "fashionable"] appearance." Less than a week later, perhaps before Gropius had even received the letter, the first parts of the foundation had been poured, and Gropius had little option left.

It must sound shockingly revisionist to those of us brought up to think of Gropius as a super-pure functionalist whose designs grew out of the *innerste Wesen* ("the inmost essence," his own words) of their being, to find him here accepting the role of a stylist, an exterior decorator, prepared to do a "skin job" on a design by another hand. It is also interesting to speculate why Werner should have so lost Benscheidt's confidence in matters of architectural and artistic taste that he was prepared to transfer what might be called the "public" aspects of the design to a different architect.

Here one can reasonably guess that his American experiences, perhaps even direct pressure from his investors at United Shoe Machinery, had convinced Benscheidt of a need to put a smarter face on the new enterprise than Werner's perfectly adequate but humdrum and old-fashioned exterior, with its thick mullions and arched window tops. To find a letter from such a well-connected and well-qualified former assistant of the great (and officially endorsed) industrial architect Peter Behrens waiting for him on his return from

Beverly may have seemed a providential deliverance from an unexpected stylistic problem. Or it may simply have rendered precise some less-defined dissatisfaction with Werner's project for the public face of a building that was clearly intended to be a model of up-to-date practice in the world's most aggressively industrializing nation.

It is only fair to inquire exactly what parts of the project were left to Gropius's talents and discretion. The drawings submitted by Gropius to the Baupolizei in September of 1911 show a reduced and economized version of the Werner plan. One bay of the single-story production sheds in the heart of the layout was eliminated, but the general disposition, dimensions, and, apparently, the structure as well remained effectively as Werner had designed them—a range of north-lit, single-story work sheds with ancillary stores across the northwestern gable ends, and beyond them a four-story warehouse with an attic story above the cornice.

The long face of the work sheds to the northeast was masked by a three-story block of offices overlooking the railroad, and this block was then turned at right angles across part of the southeastern end of the work sheds to serve as a shipping bay, etc. To match the reduction of the

Faguswerk, second phase, Gropius and Meyer, 1913–14. (Photo, Cervin Robinson)

Faguswerk, boiler house. (Photo,
Cervin Robinson)

Faguswerk, boiler house handrails.
(Photo, author)

number of work sheds, the associated rooms proposed by Werner for the dispatch department on the eastern side of the block had also been curtailed. The new Gropius facade for the office block thus ran along two of the three exposed faces of the work sheds. However, this was more than just a facade; behind the now famous glass wall ran three stories of extensively reworked office space, which may be seen as the real contribution of Gropius and his partner Adolf Meyer.

In view of Benscheidt's expressed desire to improve the appearance of the plant, this state of the design seems somewhat self-defeating, since hardly any of the new work was visible to the public. The feature originally most visible from the street entrance was a single-story element on the corner of the work sheds and about the same height. Its architectural style was simple and block-like, with small windows and a visible pitched roof. It was only in the greatly expanded second phase of the design, undertaken in 1912, completed in 1914, that Gropius and Meyer were able to extend these innovative facades as far as the public corner, where they created the famous glazed staircase and added that massively stylish entrance block "lined with darker horizontal bands of brick" in the monumental manner of Peter Behrens.

This still leaves an interesting question: why was it the least visible facade—the one overlooking the railroads—that was so extensively redesigned? One clue is that a three-story block on this side was apparently always intended as the location of the administrative offices and the drafting rooms, for they are on the Werner drawings. Drafting rooms would be seen as benefiting from copious north-light windows, such as Gropius's large-scale glazing provided. Beyond this, it appears that Benscheidt was giving himself and his managers an "American" working environment, such as he would indeed have seen in the executive block at United Shoe Machinery Corporation.

While this, no doubt, would have impressed visitors to the plant—the offices are still strikingly light and pleasant—one must assume that external image was not yet a major issue and that it was, slightly paradoxically, internal architectural aspects that were being made more tasteful or fashionable.

When the image of the visible public side of the plant did become an issue, however, Gropius and Meyer modified their facade system in a very striking manner. They added that solidly walled entrance unit, reached by a small flight of conventionally monumental steps and entered through a massively detailed door that is patterned in rivet heads. The entrance hall is crisply decorated with a system of "paneling" delineated by strips of black glass let into the white stuccoed surface. There is nothing innovatively modern about most of this; Benevolo rightly relates it to Behrens, but the remarkably elegant internal treatment seems to have more to do with the work of the widely admired Viennese masters Josef Hoffmann and Otto Wagner.

In spite of the gains in office lighting that derive from the huge expanses of glazing, the revised office wings still suffer some inexplicable defects of functional design. For instance, Gropius and Meyer eliminated most of Werner's small windows on the exposed back walls of the offices where they rise above the single-story worksheds. Since the access corridors to the offices are along these walls, they now have to be daylit with light borrowed through glazed partitions and doors along the corridors. They therefore become very dark toward the end of the work day, since the light of the western sun that would otherwise have entered them through the small windows is excluded by the solid back walls. Indeed, a close examination of the office wings reveals all the thumbprints of a young architectural practice hungry for work—not so much incompetence as persistent over-design. What separates it from American factory architecture, more than anything else, is its tendency to be clever, original, and complicated at just those points where an American builder would have availed himself of the simplest and conventionally tested solution.

The most conspicuous example of this is the battering (tapering back) of the brick piers. In terms of strict economy of building material, this is obviously correct, since the piers have less weight to carry in their upper reaches and can therefore be reduced in section. But it would have been rejected by any American builder under normal circumstances

Faguswerk, glass wall. (Photo,
Cervin Robinson)

Faguswerk, basement windows.
(Photo, author)

Faguswerk, detail of window framing, second construction phase.
(Photo, author)

because of the concomitant diseconomies of more difficult setting out of the work and the even greater diseconomies in getting it accurately built by the bricklayers. Where such reduction in section is required in American work, it is achieved by discrete steps, usually of one leaf of brickwork, thus leaving all the surfaces vertical and square. It is worth noting that for the sake of consistency, either of setting out or of aesthetic effect, all the brick surfaces on those facades at Fagus, even the aprons below the projected windows, are battered back at the same angle!

Again, the windows project only because the piers are battered, and the projection at the base is quite minimal— just 100 mm. at the bottom and increasing to about twice that at the top. Whether, as far as illumination of the interiors is concerned, anything has been gained or lost by this projected treatment of the glazing is almost impossible to assess. Where there must be a clear gain in illumination is in the elimination of Werner's thick stone mullions (though that could have been achieved without projection), and the slim metal glazing bars employed at Fagus certainly obstruct less light than the wooden industrial sash still being employed in many American Daylight factories at that time.

It is perfectly plain, as one views these visually satisfying facades with all their obsessive, fastidious, machine-style details and the optical refinements of their battered piers, that Benscheidt did indeed get what he had asked for: there is an inordinate amount of architectonics and aesthetics going on, probably more than on any other industrial structure that does not actually have period stylistic details added to it. Out of a strangely conceived program and divided architectural authorship came one of the most fascinating designs of the classic first period of the *Deutscher Werkbund,* a structure that looks forward, obliquely, to a still-unformulated architectural future but brings with it a heavy load from the past.

That past was neither remote nor traditional, but was the recent *Werkbund* past of optimism, reformist zeal, and concern for the *Durchgeistigung* (roughly, spiritualization) of German industry and its products. That past shows in all the echoes of Behrens, Wagner, and Hoffman that any tolerably well-informed visitor will recognize. But, to say it again, the design is not easy to pull apart into less modern and more modern, more original and less original. That stolidly crafted *Werkbund* door and the *Werkstatte*-Classical entrance hall behind it lead one to what must be the most original and forward-looking aspect of the whole building: the flying staircase in the glazed corner. An aesthetic and architectonic device *par excellence* (if Gropius really did convince Benscheidt that it was an economy to omit the corner column, one can only hope that they both enjoyed this structural *witz* with their tongues firmly in cheek), the glazed corner was already an impressive aesthetic innovation when applied to the original northeast corner, which has no staircase.

As one ascends a staircase that seemingly floats free within it, however, the glazed corner becomes an aesthetic experience of a totally different order. One rises into a space of increasing "modernity" until one reaches the landing at the top, which gives access to the highest of the office corridors. That space must be one of the classic locations of the modern sensibility in architecture; the landing has floor-to-ceiling glass on three sides and two glazed corners without columns—almost a decade before either Frank Lloyd Wright or R. M. Schindler had done their versions of the device in Los Angeles. It has the kind of open, limpid, *unbegrentzt* (unenclosed) space that would, in due course, become the International Style's most beguiling contribution to the vocabulary of architecture.

Industrial Architecture and Monumental Art
The Americanization of European industry and its buildings had already begun in 1900, through normal processes of capitalist technology-transfer, and needed no help from Gropius. And if the Faguswerk is not in itself an example of the Americanization of European modern architecture, it nonetheless stands near the beginning of both processes. Even if it now seems less "modern" than carefully chosen propaganda pictures have made it appear, and less American than some observers might suspect, it is still possible that

the experience of designing it and the encounters with the Benscheidts were both instrumental in turning the attention of Gropius to what was to become the revolutionary topic of the development of modern American industrial building. Whether or not Carl Benscheidt specifically directed Gropius to the topic, the once-current legend that he actually brought back from America a package of illustrations, possibly put in his hand by some representative of Atlas Portland Cement, now seems to be just that, a legend. In any case the package could not have encompassed all the illustrations to the famous article in the *Jahrbuch des Deutschen Werkbundes* of 1913, since some of the buildings shown there (such as the Continental Motors plant in Detroit) seem not to have been completed until almost two years after his return.

However, Gropius appears to have been aware of American developments by the time he gave a lecture on *Monumentale Kunst und Industriebau* for the Folkwang Museum in Hagen in April 1911, since the illustrations noted for that lecture are reported to contain examples of *Silogebäude* (though it is possible that this might have been a European example by, say, the well-known German concrete firm of Wayss und Freytag[3]). It seems clear that the real surge of interest came only later, after Fagus was in hand. Though probably not much later, however: according to Giedion, who presumably had it from Gropius himself, Gropius corresponded for a year with sources in the United States and Canada[4] for illustrations for the 1913 article. Even allowing that some of the illustrations procured were of work completed as late as 1912, the normal lead times required in the production of illustrated books and the slow pace of the transatlantic mails would probably push the beginning of that year of correspondence well back into 1911, and, possibly, into the period when the Folkwang lecture was being prepared.

The pictures seem to have come largely from the American concrete industry, a term which for convenience may be taken to include the offices of the various Kahn operations in Detroit and of the Atlas Portland Cement Company. There are a few oddities here, even so; one of the Kahn buildings (Continental Motors, again) was, as far as can be ascertained, steel framed, and at least two, possibly three, of the grain elevators were not of concrete construction. Also one must note that the quality of some of the illustrations is technically poor. They have obviously been rescreened from pictures that were already half-toned, and some parts may have been retouched as well. Just because they are such poor pictures, one cannot help wondering if these may not represent some of Gropius's original sightings of the Concrete Atlantis in trade publications, carefully preserved, since I have been told that he sometimes referred to this whole collection of pictures as if he remembered them as being "newspaper clippings." In any case these scattered sources and the year-long correspondence suggest an energetic and determined search for material. What was so compelling about these images, both to him and then later to the whole generation of modernists on whom they had so galvanic an effect?

Direct explanation is not available. His own utterances about America up to and including 1913 are very few indeed. On the other hand, he lectured and wrote on industrial architecture fairly extensively and in the process left a small number of oblique indications of what could have inspired his interest in the buildings of the *Mutterland der Industrie*. His purely professional motives in making himself such a visible expert on industrial architecture can be surmised without reference to these texts: sooner or later he would have to get out from under the shadow of Behrens and the *Werkbund* establishment. However useful the great man's name and the organizational connection might be in getting him started (and he was ever careful of such matters), his credibility in the long term would require an independent basis. (By 1913 he could, apparently, be counted among the *Werkbund's* more dissident younger members.[5]) He apparently set out to achieve this independent position by taking his stand on two innovative intellectual positions: a close reading of recent writings on aesthetics and an appeal to the industrial prestige of the United States.

His reliance on recent writings on aesthetics is evident in the opening paragraphs of his Folkwang lecture:

Let me venture, straight away, to put forward a few fundamental propositions of a general nature on monumental art, related in part to the new art historical perceptions of Riegl and Worringer, as basic matters for later consideration.[6]

A debt to Wilhelm Worringer in Gropius's views on industrial architecture has often been supposed, though with little more textual "proof" than that they both availed themselves of comparisons between America and ancient Egypt. However, Worringer did not make the comparison directly in print until 1927, in *Ägyptische Kunst,* and in doing so he may have been influenced by younger modernists, since he uses an illustration that had first appeared in Gropius's 1913 article! More striking still, he uses a version that had been somewhat altered by Le Corbusier. And the quotation about "the Americanism you otherwise despise" that opened this section of the book appeared only in a rather combative special introduction to the English translation of *Ägyptische Kunst* which appeared over a year later.[7]

When Gropius does make his Egyptian connection, it clearly does derive from Worringer, but it is patched together out of ideas from Worringer's first book, *Abstraktion und Einfühlung (Abstraction and Empathy),* which was something of an intellectual sensation in Germany when it came out in 1908, just in time to affect Gropius's thinking as he was setting out on his independent career. What he claims to derive from Worringer, and from Alois Riegl (who is one of Worringer's avowed sources), turns out as follows:

Art is made by man and for man; it is a contradiction of nature. It seeks to change the absolute beauty proper to nature, into conscious relative beauty. This conversion is wrought by the will. What is without will in nature, man strives to affect by means of the will. At the power center of man's will stand two innate drives: to know and to create. With these he takes hold of the sensual and transcendental world of phenomena. While the creative drive responds to the mechanical constraints of things and phenomena, its being is life-affirming, generative, and construc-

tive, but directs that the drive to knowledge of the phenomenal world be life-denying, critical, destructive. Both strive, in a final ideal resolution, to come together.

Material as such is dead and without being, until life gives it form and the creative will of the artist shapes it. "In this paper, in this stone," said Michelangelo, "will be no meaning that I do not put there." Will thus orders chaos, renders the arbitrary necessary, and the disorderly rhythmic. . . . The value of a work of art stands first in the spiritual satisfaction of an inner need for resolution, less in the quality of its materials. For creator and spectator alike, the work of art reveals a pacification of the confusions of the world.[8]

Much of this would be familiar stuff, if still fairly fresh, in the years immediately following the publication of *Abstraktion und Einfühlung.* Furthermore, Gropius contrives to pick up or anticipate a number of ideas and attitudes that can be compared to the demands for the *Durchgeistigung* (which meant so much more to concerned Germans than just "spiritualization") of all the products of craft and industry that were made by Hermann Muthesius at the *Werkbund's* annual conference in that same year of 1911. Gropius, however, is more direct than Muthesius in taking his *Kunstwollen* out into the world of industrial design and production:

All material things are no more than serviceable aids, with which everyday sensory impressions can reach higher mental states, even become artistic drives. . . . Art needs belief in some great common idea with which to achieve the heights. To receive a deep impression from a building, we must have belief in the idea that it presents.

Today we see signs that our great technical and scientific epoch will be followed by a time of inwardness. Civilization will be succeeded by culture. . . . Work must be established in palaces that give the workman, now a slave to industrial labor, not only light, air, and hygiene, but also an indication of the great common idea that drives everything. Only then can the individual submit to the impersonal without losing the joy of working together for that greater common good previously unattainable by a single individual. This awareness in every worker could even

*ward off the kind of social catastrophe that seems to be brew-
ing daily in our present economic system. Farsighted managers
have long known that with the satisfaction of individual workers,
the common work spirit also grows, and with it the efficiency of
the whole plant. The sophisticated calculations of the industri-
alist will take all profitable steps to relieve the deadening monotony of factory work and alleviate its constraints. That is, he
will attend not only to light, air, and cleanliness in the design of
his buildings and work spaces, but will also take cognizance of
those basic sentiments of beauty that even uneducated workers
possess.*

*Modern living needs new building organisms expressing the life
forms of our times—stations, department stores, factories all
demand a uniquely modern expression that cannot be satis-
fied in the styles of centuries past without falling into empty
schematics or period fancy-dress. Instead of the application of
superficial formulas, an inward shaping of these new architectural problems is required, non-routine thinking, an aesthetic reconsideration of the basic forms of former times, not added
decoration. The proportioning of the building masses is the highest task (and foundation) of architecture; ornament is only a
final touch. . . . Exactly expressed form, free of all accidental
effects, clear contrasts, orderly articulation in the arrangement
of every part, and unity of form and color, these are the ground
rules of the rhythmics of modern architectural design.*[9]

Like most of the architecture of Gropius at this period,
this text, with its lists of current duties and modern materials, is well informed, up-to-the-minute, and somewhat derivative. Its apparent lack of illuminating originality is more than
compensated for by a rewarding absence of that all-too-fre-
quent, all-too-heavy consciousness of the important part that
architectonic culture should play in the "Manifest Destiny" of
the German *Volk*—a rhetoric that infests the utterances of
Hermann Muthesius and other senior mouthpieces of the
Werkbund in those years. Instead there is a certain bustling
approach to a number of jobs to be done in reforming factory design and enhancing the social performance of architecture in that field.

It also gives a clear hint of the frame of mind that enabled Gropius to engage in the purely "architectonic, aesthetic" improvement of Werner's design for Fagus. In light of this argument, that task could be seen as worthy because of its importance to the "common work spirit," to enhanced production, and to the possible prevention of some social catastrophe brewing daily in the capitalist system of industrial production. It is easy, nowadays, to doubt cynically that factory architecture has ever given any production-line worker the slightest sense of belonging to any larger social enterprise governed by some great common idea, yet the propositions put forward here by Gropius are not so different from those that can be found in American writings about the value of good architecture in industrial plants.[10] This should not be surprising; conscious emulation of one great industrial power by another had already led to the foundation of the giant concern Allgemeine Elektrizitäts Gesellschaft (AEG for short), the German General Electric Corporation, which employed the talents of Peter Behrens. The same kind of thinking at a parochial, rather than national, scale had led to the formation of Fagus, which employed the talents of Gropius himself. Again, it is intriguing to speculate what Gropius may have learned, even indirectly, from Benscheidt about American ideas of better relations with the work force.

Yet there is strikingly little that refers directly to America or to American industrial practices in the text of the Folkwang lecture as we have it. Such references are sparse throughout his writings of the period, in spite of the crucial role he played in introducing these matters into the world of European architecture. Even in the celebrated article in the *Jahrbuch* that launched the whole train of Americanizing developments, "Die Entwicklung Moderner Industriebaukunst," the references to America come only in the closing paragraphs and are nowhere textually linked to the illustrations that were to have such a profound effect on the architectural ideas of his contemporaries.

The earlier parts of the *Jahrbuch* article effectively repeat the kinds of arguments that had been offered in the Folkwang Museum lecture, though couched in a more expansive rhetoric that propounds his own version of the accepted *Werkbund* propaganda that "Good Design is Good Business":

The experience of a number of firms has shown quite plainly that it pays in the long run to give thought to the artistic worth as well as the technical perfection and saleability of a product, because their goods have become a means of carrying tastefulness and quality among large numbers of the people. Not only have they earned themselves a reputation for promoting culture but, which is equally important in business, have considerably increased their pecuniary gain.[11]

Much of what follows repeats the material set out in the Folkwang lecture, sometimes almost verbatim, sometimes more elaborately:

A worker will find that a room well thought out by an artist, which responds to the innate sense of beauty we all possess, will relieve the monotony of the daily task and he will be more willing to join in the common enterprise. If the worker is happy, he will take more pleasure in his duties, and the productivity of the firm will increase.[12]

After this comes a series of encomiums on those German companies that had heeded or inspired such advice and had employed architects like Hans Poelzig, Heinz Stoffregen, and Martin Wagner, and above all, Peter Behrens. His buildings for the AEG, being based "simply . . . on the elementary principles of architectonics," are *Denkmaler von Adel und Kraft* (monuments of nobility and strength), "commanding their surroundings with truly classical grandeur and which no-one can pass by without being involved emotionally."[13] Adding all these virtues together at the end of the penultimate paragraph of the article, Gropius declares that the works of architects such as these

convey the impression of a coherent architecture which has at last discovered the right dress for the life style of the times and firmly rejects the romantic residue of past styles as cowardly and unreal.[14]

At this point he could properly have stopped, having written a dutifully persuasive article, well composed and up-to-date in its references, embracing all the liberal and progressive viewpoints on trade, industry, and design then in good currency, and concluding on the required note of hortatory optimism. But then comes the final paragraph, which has no necessary or direct connection with what has come before and moves the whole argument into much more exotic territory. It introduces an independent, not to say radical, note that had not appeared in the preceding paragraphs:

Compared to the rest of Europe, Germany seems to have taken a considerable stride ahead in the field of artistic factory building, but America, the Motherland of Industry, possesses some majestic original constructions which far outstrip anything of a similar kind achieved in Germany. The compelling monumentality of the Canadian and South American grain elevators, the coaling bunkers built for the leading railway companies and the newest work halls of the great North American industrial trusts can almost bear comparison with the work of the ancient Egyptians in their overwhelming monumental power. Their unique individuality is so unmistakable that the meaning of the structure becomes abundantly clear to the passer-by. But the impact of these buildings does not depend on sheer material size alone. That is certainly not where to look for an explanation of their monumental originality. It seems to lie rather in the fact that American builders have retained a natural feeling for large compact forms fresh and intact. Our own architects might take this as a valuable hint and refuse to pay any more attention to those fits of historicist nostalgia and other intellectual fancies under which European creativity still labors and which frustrate our true artistic naiveté.[15]

This, suddenly, seems to be the tone of architectural polemics of the 1920s and anticipates Le Corbusier's frequent use of America as a term of comparison that finds Europe wanting. This was not a total innovation, of course; Adolf Loos had done it throughout his polemics after returning to Vienna from America at the turn of the century. Furthermore, the world of German architecture (and that of the rest of Europe to a lesser extent) had been prepared for the idea of looking to America for significant innovation by the publication of the two celebrated Wasmuth volumes

Last paragraph of "Die Entwicklung Moderner Industriebaukunst," by Walter Gropius in *Jahrbuch des Deutschen Werkbundes*, 1913. (Courtesy of Avery Library, Columbia University)

Im Vergleich mit den übrigen Ländern Europas scheint Deutschland auf dem Gebiete des künstlerischen Fabrikbaus einen Vorsprung gewonnen zu haben. Aber im Mutterlande der Industrie, in Amerika, sind industrielle Groß= bauten entstanden, deren ungekannte Majestät auch unsere besten deutschen Bauten dieser Gattung überragt. Die Getreidesilos von Kanada und Süd= amerika, die Kohlensilos der großen Eisenbahnlinien und die modernsten Werkhallen der nordamerikanischen Industrietrusts halten in ihrer monumen= talen Gewalt des Eindrucks fast einen Vergleich mit den Bauten des alten Ägyptens aus. Sie tragen ein architektonisches Gesicht von solcher Bestimmt= heit, daß dem Beschauer mit überzeugender Wucht der Sinn des Gehäuses eindeutig begreiflich wird. Die Selbstverständlichkeit dieser Bauten beruht nun nicht auf der materiellen Überlegenheit ihrer Größenausdehnungen — hierin ist der Grund monumentaler Wirkung gewiß nicht zu suchen — viel= mehr scheint sich bei ihren Erbauern der natürliche Sinn für große, knapp ge= bundene Form, selbständig, gesund und rein erhalten zu haben. Darin liegt aber ein wertvoller Hinweis für uns, den historischen Sehnsüchten und den anderen Bedenken intellektueller Art, die unser modernes europäisches Kunst= schaffen trüben und künstlerischer Naivität im Wege sind, für immer die Ach= tung zu versagen.

on Frank Lloyd Wright in 1910 and 1911.[16] Gropius, indeed, was the first German architect to show clear influence from Wright, in the towers of the *Werkbund* pavilion at the Cologne exhibition of 1914, the design for which must have been in hand before this article was published. Loos, of course, had also put engineers among those, like peasants, who could only build well and in the style of their own time because they knew no other.[17]

But Gropius introduces his American builders at a very high level; the passage abounds in strong adjectives of approval, as Karin Wilhelm has observed in her study *Walter Gropius Industriearchitekt.*[18] No wonder these paragons of architectural virtue are offered as models to our architects, who should "take this as a valuable hint," abandon their intellectual and historicizing errors, and rediscover their "true artistic naiveté." There is an important shift of attitude implied here; for the previous generation, engineers, if approved at all, had been "our Hellenes," in the famous phrase of Adolf Loos.[19] Gropius, however, removes them from the pinnacle of approved high-classical culture that is implied by the Hellenic comparison and presents them instead as the newer kind of artist-hero, the noble savage.

This radical view of engineers had been advanced in the preceding years by, most notably, the Italian Futurist F. T. Marinetti, with his talk of "men of the people without culture or education, who are nevertheless endowed with what I call the gift of mechanical prophecy, the flair for metals."[20] But these engineers of Gropius have the added authority of coming from the Motherland of Industry, the American lands where Europeans had first discovered what they believed to be noble savages, unspoiled peoples who had retained those human virtues that sophisticated Europe had mislaid.

Since such ideas had gained some currency in cultured circles in Germany, Gropius was to some extent preaching to the converted. But he had armed himself with a new device to persuade those not yet converted, provided they were *au courant* with the rest of the latest theories of art history: the Egyptian comparison, which taps a reservoir of rather specific concepts that had not been deployed in this kind of argument before. It seems to come from a close, perceptive, and rather ingenious reading of *Abstraktion und Einfühlung*, whose enthusiastic reception (even before publication, according to Worringer himself) ensured that its assumptions, arguments, and combative conclusions would be known in some fashion to Gropius's more educated German readers. The elements of Worringer's thought that he employed can be found among passages such as the following:

The artistic volition of savage peoples, in so far as they possess any at all, then the artistic volition of all primitive epochs of art . . . exhibit this abstract tendency. This urge to abstraction stands at the beginning of every art. . . . The style most perfect in its regularity, the style of the highest abstraction, most strict in its exclusion of life, is peculiar to the peoples at the most primitive cultural level. A causal connection must therefore exist between primitive culture and the highest, purest regular art-form.[21]

One can see here the concepts that Gropius would develop into his propositions about American builders being able to create the large, compact, compellingly monumental forms of the grain elevators because they had retained their artistic naiveté fresh and intact. Some thirty pages later in Worringer comes the hook connecting the ancient Egyptians to this kind of argumentation:

It may be stated here . . . that of all the ancient cultural peoples the Egyptians carried through most intensively the abstract tendency in artistic volition.[22]

Less than a dozen lines later is a citation from Alois Riegl to the effect that in Egyptian art,

wherever possible, the line was drawn absolutely straight, in response to a marked tendency toward maximum crystalline regularity in the composition; where deviations from the straight were unavoidable, they were incorporated in a curve that was as regular as possible. The beauty of these Egyptian works of art rests in the strict proportionality of the parts and in their domination by the unity of undivided and unbroken outlines.[23]

Given that, for both Worringer and Riegl, "the perfect example of the Egyptian artistic volition is the pyramid,"[24] one must wonder if Gropius had also tapped into that older tradition, both marginally Christian and (apparently) Masonic—to which Katharine Marling drew attention in her study of Charles Demuth's famous grain-elevator painting *My Egypt*[25]—which held that the pyramids were granaries where the grain from the seven fat years was stored at the behest of the Israelite Joseph, as recounted in the Book of Genesis. Ultimately, however, the most crucial part of his debt to Worringer must lie in the passage, which Worringer himself describes as an "audacious comparison," that links modern scientific man, with his rationalistic cognition, back to the instinctual responses of man at his most primitive:

It is as though the instinct for "the thing in itself" (Ding an Sich) were most powerful in primitive man. Increasing spiritual mastery of the outside world and habituation to it means a blunting and dimming of this instinct. Only after the human spirit has passed, in thousands of years of its evolution along the whole course of rationalistic cognition, does the feeling for "the thing in itself" reawaken as the final resolution of knowledge. That which was previously instinct is now the ultimate product of cognition.[26]

Grain elevators in Montreal and
Fort William. (From *Jahrbuch des
Deutschen Werkbundes*, 1913; cour-
tesy Avery Library, Columbia
University)

Dakota Elevator, Buffalo, New
York, and Bunge y Born Elevator,
Buenos Aires, Argentina. (*Jahrbuch
des Deutschen Werkbundes,* 1913)

Grain elevators in South America
and at Bahia Blanca, Argentina.
(*Jahrbuch des Deutschen Werkbundes*, 1913)

Washburn-Crosby silos in Buffalo,
New York, and Minneapolis, Minnesota; silo of the Baltimore and
Ohio railroad in Baltimore, Maryland. (*Jahrbuch des Deutschen Werkbundes,* 1913)

United States Printing Co., Cincinnati, Ohio, and Ford Motor Company plant Detroit, Michigan. (*Jahrbuch des Deutschen Werkbundes*, 1913)

Continental Motor Manufacturing Company plant, Detroit, Michigan. (*Jahrbuch des Deutschen Werkbundes*, 1913)

Alling and Corry and Roth Packing
Company warehouses, Cincinnati,
Ohio. (*Jahrbuch des Deutschen
Werkbundes*, 1913)

Grain elevator, Worms, Germany,
by Wayss und Freytag, 1908. (From
Bauten der Arbeit und des Werkehrs,
1929)

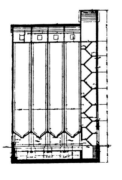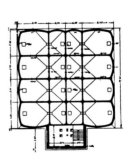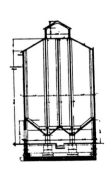

Grain elevator, Worms, plan and
section. (From *Bauten der Arbeit und
des Werkehrs,* 1929)

Grain silo, Barby an der Elbe, Germany, by Wayss und Freytag, 1922. (From *Bauten der Arbeit und des Werkehrs*, 1929)

As a rhetorical trope, Gropius's implicit evocation of the supposed primitivism of American builders was extremely timely. Those of his generation, like the Futurist painter Umberto Boccioni, who claimed to be "the primitives of a new sensibility" could see themselves and their mechanistic enthusiasms given monumental status in Gropius's words and even more so in the seven pages of his illustrations of factories and elevators, which—by some quirk of make-up and binding—gained impact and importance by appearing before the article and without explanation. On the generation at large, the impact was considerable, as the numerous imitations and citations in subsequent writings and drawings attest. What is little noted, however, was the parallel effect that the new American designs, particularly for elevators, was having on European engineers, presumably for "objective" functional reasons that supposedly did not involve rhetoric or aesthetics. The evidence of this has been plain to see, not only in the form of grain elevators and occasional factories that follow American patterns, but also in the more popular literature of architecture. The first volume of Walter Müller-Wülckow's *Blauen Bucher* series, which dealt only with the architecture of work and transport and which by the printing of 1929 had reached an edition of fifty-thousand copies, shows on facing pages[27] two grain elevators by the famous concrete company of Wayss und Freytag. The earlier, of 1908, has a rusticated basement and a doubled "pediment" made by its headworks. Its plan, as shown in the appendix to the volume, is square, compact, and remarkably elegant, using curved diaphragm walls of subtly tapered thinness and grouping its bins in a symmetrical array that looks like nothing so much as a cluster of soap bubbles. On the facing page is another example, this time from 1922–24, which has its ranked cylindrical bins arranged in two parallel rows in a format and under headworks that would have passed unnoticed in Minneapolis or Buffalo by that time. The notes below the caption remark specifically that its (allegedly) unconventional design is *nach amerikanischen Vorbild*—on the American model.

Whatever might be happening in the "real" world of engineering, however, Gropius seems to have produced a crucial change in the sensibilities of modern architects, bringing together a set of images whose time had come in the development of European architectural sensibility and a set of arguments—or, at least, verbal formulae—that may or may not have "explained" those images, but did offer a language by which they could be incorporated into the general body of architectural discourse. The stage was set for the legitimization, so to speak, of industrial forms as the basic vocabulary of modernism. The upheavals of the Great War were to intervene, but also gave time for their assimilation; and when the war was over, they were at hand as elements of architectural composition and as the terminology of architectural polemic.

Reminders to Architects

In spite of the doubts that have been expressed about the "American" aspects of the Faguswerk, it does make one appearance in the early modernist literature that implies that it *is* American, perhaps even *in* America. This was in some early editions and translations of Le Corbusier's *Vers une Architecture,* which appeared in book form in 1923. In the second of the three chapters headed "Rappels à MM. les Architectes," which extols the virtues of "American factories," Fagus appears, uncaptioned, among a number of other uncaptioned illustrations of buildings that are undoubtedly American factories.[28] This may only have been a mistake or aberration—in other editions and translations it is replaced by an illustration of Ford's Old Shop at Highland Park—but it suggests that Le Corbusier's arguments may have been less concerned with logical, objective persuasion than with other matters.

In this, of course, he follows in a tradition already established by the rhetoric of the Futurists and even Gropius himself, to whom Le Corbusier was indebted for more than just illustrations. Since it was Le Corbusier who was the ultimate propagandist for American industrial buildings as the models for modern architecture, it is worthwhile to review the route he had followed in coming to this position, and to see what had changed from the position established by Gropius before the war.

The first, though rather enigmatic, of these differences is Le Corbusier's commitment to reinforced concrete as the building material of the future. Though this is not overtly an issue in the chapters of *Vers une Architecture* that concern us here, his illustrations are almost exclusively of concrete structures and, curiously, are all implicitly of North American buildings rather than those of the European concrete tradition, with which he was well acquainted. His interest in concrete had begun well before the war, and he had been one of a group in his native La Chaux de Fonds that was promoting patentable concrete construction systems (Monol, Domino) as well as translating the textbooks of Ernst Mörsch, head of engineering at the Berlin concrete firm of Wayss und Freytag.

Furthermore, he had worked, however briefly, for Auguste Perret, who was then (1908) entering on his greatest fame as an architect and engineer in reinforced concrete, and he seems to have rejoined the circle around Perret when he returned to Paris permanently in 1917. He was also well acquainted with the work of other French engineers, like Freyssinet and Hennebique, whose reputations were founded on their work in concrete. Apart from Freyssinet, however, whose work appears in the closing pages of *Vers une Architecture,* the book conspicuously ignores the achievements of the European concrete tradition.

Yet at the time these chapters were originally published, as articles in the magazine *L'Esprit Nouveau* in 1920, these European concrete architects and engineers had produced a body of work—industrial and civic—that could have convincingly illustrated the points that Le Corbusier wished to make about "volume" and "surface" in the "Rappels à MM. les Architectes." There may have been local, contingent, and possibly painful reasons why he did not use their work; he was in the throes of a major quarrel with Auguste Perret, for instance, and nearly all the local heroes were, to some extent, compromised in his view by having collaborated with architects of the former Art Nouveau or Beaux-Arts styles. This, again, would apply *a fortiori* to Perret, whose work nearly always shows classicizing tendencies that might well make it look irresolute by comparison with the austere and powerful forms that had been revealed in Gropius's illustrations of 1913.

Indeed, Le Corbusier's reuse of many (though not all) of the Gropius illustrations is a most telling tribute to the talismanic, if not mythic, power that these images had already attained. The power was not only in the images themselves, it is clear; it derived also from their usefulness as illustrations to the theme of the modern noble savage that Gropius had attached to them. But Le Corbusier raises this theme to a far higher pitch. The tone of his writing in the *rappels* often matches the pugnacity of prewar Futurist manifestoes, and is made more memorable (especially to architects) by being delivered in short aphoristic paragraphs deliberately recalling those of the great *Histoire de l'Architecture* of Auguste Choisy (1894), the standard text on which Le Corbusier's generation had been raised. This, no doubt, helped to establish the historical dimension crucial to his argument, but the rest of the argument has few precedents in either style or content.

The three *rappels,* or "Reminders to Architects," are, in order, "Volume," "Surface," and "Plan," and they form the first separately subtitled section of the book. However, they are preceded by an introductory chapter titled "The Engineer's Aesthetic and Architecture," which brings the noble savage concept significantly to the fore and establishes the necessary terms of reference for the reading of "Volume," "Surface," and all other parts of the book that depend on the notion of technological progress.

The fundamental concepts are, for instance, the need for "truth," that "we no longer have the money to erect historical reminiscences," or that architecture is "a product of happy peoples and a thing which in itself produces happy peoples." In this context engineers are apostrophized twice in this chapter. On one occasion they are praised as followers of the laws of nature rather than of aesthetic fancies:

Our engineers produce architecture, for they employ a mathematical calculation which derives from natural law, and these works give us a feeling of Harmony. . . . Now, in handling a mathematical problem, a man is regarding it from a purely abstract point of view, and in such a state, his taste must follow a sure and certain path.[29]

This does not refer directly to Worringer, although the use of the work "abstract" in the context of engineering suggests a clear connection with the Gropius version of the Worringer argument, but engineers are here also clearly meant to be construed as, in some degree, the equivalents of noble savages, at least in contrast to architects, who are dismissed as "disillusioned, unemployed, boastful and peevish." Engineers, by contrast, had made their other appearance in this chapter as "Healthy and virile, active and useful, balanced and happy in their work."[30]

As a former engineer myself I am inclined to regard this passage cynically and to wonder how Le Corbusier could be so naive, or so driven by polemical zeal, as to propose it. However, the most significant issue in this paragraph is a shift in the meaning of that crucial word "abstract" as applied to the art of "primitives." Worringer clearly had not intended it to mean undecorated, and in this he is at one with Adolf Loos, whose primitives decorated everything they could lay their hands on. But Loos had proposed that such decorative compulsions were improper in a normal, modern twentieth-century culture. Consequently, the inclination of self-consciously modern architects between about 1910 and 1930 was to separate, and even oppose, the abstract and the ornamental and to admire only the abstract that is free of ornament. Under the dispensation established by Worringer's "audacious comparison"—in which both primitives and sophisticates are properly in touch with the *Ding an Sich*—the art of the truly and valuably primitive, including American engineers and others of that healthy, virile, active, useful, balanced, and happy breed, will be as abstract and as free of ornamentation as an Egyptian pyramid.

Even though Le Corbusier's magazine *L'Esprit Nouveau* had printed a truncated French translation of Loos's *Ornament und Verbrechen* even before *Vers une Architecture* was published, the contents and illustrations of the two *rappels* under consideration here must still be regarded chiefly as an extension of Gropius's argument in the 1913 article. Of the nine illustrations of grain elevators shown in the first *rappel*, "Le Volume," the four largest, best known, and most strategically placed are all from the *Jahrbuch* article. None of the seven factories that illustrate the second *rappel*, "La Surface," had previously appeared in the *Jahrbuch* article, but since the Fagus factory does, one must wonder whether it was well enough known for Le Corbusier's readers to identify it as something different from the other illustrations or whether they might have been deceived—even deliberately deceived.

In the case of this one small illustration, the deception may not be grievous; but in the context of the illustrations to the *rappels* as a whole, Le Corbusier's manipulation of the imagery must be addressed, since it seems to be part and parcel of his polemical method. As Paul Turner was the first to point out in print, though it had long been known to the gossips, Le Corbusier *cheats*.[32] Two of the illustrations borrowed from Gropius have been altered, as has the picture of the Ford plant that replaces that of the Faguswerk. With one illustration it is difficult to see what he has gained: the removal of the dome of the old Marché Bon Secours from the lower right-hand corner of the view of the Government 1 elevator in Montreal does nothing to clarify the image[33] and, indeed, deprives him of a chance to make an easy contrast between the clean and new and the depraved and old-fashioned.

The other two seem to reveal a serious attempt to tamper with the evidence of the buildings themselves, to bring them closer to his aesthetic preferences. Both have been given a flatter skyline—the Ford plant by obscuring the little turrets above the staircases at intervals along its immense facade, and the tremendous tile-built Bunge y Born elevator in Buenos Aires (which he miscaptions as "Canadian") by impresses the most brutal instincts by its objectivity; it calls into play the highest faculties by its very abstraction. Architectural abstraction has this about it which is magnificently peculiar to itself, that while it is rooted in hard fact it spiritualizes it, because the naked fact is nothing more than the materialization of a possible idea. The naked fact is a medium for ideas only by reason of the "order" that is applied to it. The emotions that architecture arouses spring from physical conditions which are inevitable, irrefutable and to-day forgotten.

Mass and surface are the elements by which architecture manifests itself.

Mass and surface are determined by the plan. The plan is the generator. So much the worse for those who lack imagination!

CANADIAN GRAIN STORES AND ELEVATORS

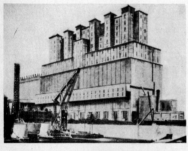

AMERICAN GRAIN STORES AND ELEVATORS

FIRST REMINDER: MASS

Architecture is the masterly, correct and magnificent play of masses brought together in light. Our eyes are made to see forms in light; light and shade reveal these forms; cubes, cones, spheres, cylinders or pyramids are the great primary forms which light reveals to advantage; the image of these is distinct and tangible within us and without ambiguity. It is for that reason that these are *beautiful forms, the most beautiful forms*. Everybody is agreed as to that, the child, the savage and the metaphysician. It is of the very nature of the plastic arts.

Egyptian, Greek or Roman architecture is an architecture of prisms, cubes and cylinders, pyramids or spheres: the Pyramids, the Temple of Luxor, the Parthenon, the Coliseum, Hadrian's Villa.

Grain elevators. (From *Towards a New Architecture*)

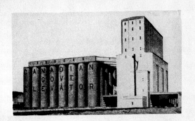

Gothic architecture is not, fundamentally, based on spheres, cones and cylinders. Only the nave is an expression of a simple form, but of a complex geometry of the second order (intersecting arches). It is for that reason that a cathedral is not very beautiful and that we search in it for compensations of a subjective kind outside plastic art. A cathedral interests us as the ingenious solution of a difficult problem, but a problem of which the postulates have been badly stated beçause they do not proceed from the great primary forms. *The cathedral is not a plastic work; it is a drama; a fight against the force of gravity, which is a sensation of a sentimental nature.*

The Pyramids, the Towers of Babylon, the Gates of Samarkand, the Parthenon, the Coliseum, the Pantheon, the Pont du Gard, Santa Sophia, the Mosques of Stamboul, the Tower

of Pisa, the Cupolas of Brunelleschi and of Michael Angelo, the Pont-Royal, the Invalides—all these belong to Architecture.

The Gare du Quai d'Orsay, the Grand Palais do not belong to Architecture.

The *architects* of to-day, lost in the sterile backwaters of their plans, their foliage, their pilasters and their lead roofs, have never acquired the conception of primary masses. They were never taught that at the Schools.

Not in pursuit of an architectural idea, but simply guided by the results of calculation (derived from the principles which govern our universe) and the conception of A LIVING ORGANISM, *the* ENGINEERS *of to-day make use of the primary elements and, by co-ordinating them in accordance with the rules, provoke in us architectural emotions and thus make the work of man ring in unison with universal order.*

Thus we have the American grain elevators and factories, the magnificent FIRST-FRUITS *of the new age.* THE AMERICAN ENGINEERS OVERWHELM WITH THEIR CALCULATIONS OUR EXPIRING ARCHITECTURE.

whiting out every one of its numerous pediments.[34] These erasures are clearly programmatic: though the pediments do not seem to have troubled Gropius, in spite of his aversion to "historicist nostalgia," they were too obviously reminiscent of ancient styles to gibe with Le Corbusier's opening proposition at the beginning of the *rappels*.

Architecture has nothing to do with the various styles, he asserts, and beyond that, he clearly wants nothing to do with anything that might be construed as superficial or decorative:

Architecture has graver ends, capable of the sublime it impresses the most brutal instincts by its objectivity; it calls into play the highest faculties by its very abstraction. Architectural abstraction has this about it which is magnificently peculiar to itself, that while it is rooted in fact, it spiritualises it. . . .

The emotions that architecture arouses spring from physical conditions which are inevitable, irrefutable and today forgotten.

Mass and surface are the elements by which architecture manifests itself. Mass and surface are generated by the plan. The plan is the generator. So much the worse for those who lack imagination.[35]

Mass, surface, and plan are indeed the topics of the three *rappels,* but the treatment of "plan" is strikingly different from that of the first two topics. No modern, primitive industrial structures appear among its illustrations. Rather, there are axonometrics and plans from Choisy's *Histoire* to carry the burden of the first part of the chapter, while layouts and perspectives from Tony Garnier's visionary *Cité Industrielle* and from Le Corbusier's own urbanistic projects do the visual work in the much longer second part of the argument, which is entirely concerned with applicable solutions to current city-planning concerns. The two preceding "industrial" *rappels* have no "applications" content of this sort; they are pure statements about the nature of architecture, but of a quite different order from what he is trying to say about the plan.

The plan had been traditionally regarded as the very essence of good architecture (indeed this was still effective dogma in most architecture schools) and was regarded in Le

Corbusier's circle as a kind of *secret professionnel* which architects understood and the lay public could not. It seems as if Le Corbusier, having discovered in American industrial buildings what he was compelled to regard as two other essential secrets behind mere appearance and style, wished to incorporate them in his philosophy but had to make them subordinate to the plan (the "generator") because he knew no other way of dealing with them without abandoning the essential secret of being an architect. Yet he presents them *before* the plan, as if they were such important discoveries that they must claim priority.

First comes "Le Volume" ("Mass" in the standard English text by Frederick Etchells). Its text is very short, barely five hundred words, but it is couched in the author's highest rhetorical vein and opens with the most resounding and well-remembered of all Le Corbusier's pronouncements on his subject:

Architecture is the masterly, correct and magnificent play of masses brought together in light. Our eyes are made to see forms in light; light and shade reveal these forms: cubes, cones, spheres, cylinders or pyramids are the great primary forms which light reveals to advantage; the image of these is distinct and tangible within us and without ambiguity. It is for that reason that these are beautiful forms, the most beautiful forms. *Everybody is agreed as to that, the child, the savage and the metaphysician. It is of the very nature of the plastic arts.*[36]

If the reader looks around for visible confirmation of these resounding fundamentalist claims, all that will be seen are pictures of grain elevators, most notably Government 1 in Montreal and the Dakota in Buffalo, which between them occupy the whole of the facing page. They serve to underwrite this intellectual leap backward from Worringer's "audacious comparison" (in which "the savage and the metaphysician" are now made to agree) to the pure geometrical solids (cubes, cones, cylinders, etc.) of Plato's *Philebus*, such as "are made by a lathe or the carpenter's rule and square" and are "always beautiful in their very nature."[37] The elevators are here made to reveal a demonstrable truth about the nature of architecture and to guarantee the truth of the argument by presenting *visual* evidence, which for most architects is more convincing than logic.

On the next page, after a passing demolition of Gothic architecture—"a cathedral," we are told, "is not very beautiful"—and equal contumely for present-day architects—"lost in the backwaters of their plans, their foliage, their pilasters"—grain elevators and factories are made the guarantors not only of the truth of architecture, but, in the two concluding paragraphs, the Laws of the Universe as well:

Not in pursuit of an architectural idea, but simply guided by the results of calculation (derived from the principles which govern our Universe) and the conception of A LIVING ORGANISM, *the* ENGINEERS *of today make use of the primary elements and, by co-ordinating them in accordance with the rules provoke in us architectural emotions and thus make the work of man ring in unison with the universal order.*

Thus we have the American grain elevators and factories, the magnificent FIRST FRUITS *of the new age.* THE AMERICAN ENGINEERS OVERWHELM WITH THEIR CALCULATIONS OUR EXPIRING ARCHITECTURE.[38]

The rhetorical capital letters and italics in this passage are Le Corbusier's own; they are in all editions and all standard translations, and they suggest a desperate need to persuade his readership of the truth of his message. And, again, if the reader seeks confirmation of these high-flown tropes, there on the facing page is another elevator, not identified by Le Corbusier, but now known to be outside Calgary, Alberta. An elevator is once more a guarantor of truth. However, it seems likely that the claim of truth is reinforced by a hidden persuader of sorts that underpins both of these *rappels*: the nature of the "Phileban" solids—cylinder, sphere, cone, etc.—which are the very essence of the discipline whereby engineers (according to Le Corbusier) "make the work of man ring in unison with the universal order."

These primary forms are generated, according to Plato, by some of the same instruments as those by which architects practice their trade: the rule, the compass, and the square. Even if they did not know that particular quotation from

Plato (though it appeared fairly frequently in aesthetic writings about abstract art in those years), architects would certainly feel at home with these forms that are such close kin to those they set out on their drawing boards. In the same vein, the axiomatically "irrefutable" rules of Euclidean geometry and the "inevitable" laws of structural statics were the "physical conditions" under which their designing would unavoidably be done. The whole passage would "ring in unison" with the customary practices and most ingrained prejudices of the architectural profession; those raised in the ineffable (or, at least, unspoken) value systems of that profession could not feel anything but flattered by their closeness to the harmonies of the universe—once the shock of seeing the flattery validated by such unprecedented structures had worn off.

To be frank, that shock has not completely worn off even now. There is still something disturbingly bold about this conflation of the crudely functional and the universally abstract. It is the kind of boldness that is the very essence of modernist sensibility, and it seems to have ensured these arguments, these images, an enduring validity and an extraordinarily long life beyond the polemical needs of the time when they were first produced. The images have come to represent canonical or exemplary structures, much as the Maison Carré or Bramante's Tempietto were exemplary designs for earlier generations. More impressive, however, is the way that *Vers une Architecture* has also made them the permanent canonical images of grain elevators, apparently preferred by those, like Vincent Scully a half-century later, who could easily have access to photographs of real-life examples from close at hand but used one of Le Corbusier's altered borrowings from Gropius instead.

The first *rappel* is probably the high point of the whole tradition of the Concrete Atlantis. Everything after it, even inside the pages of *Vers une Architecture,* is something of an anticlimax, although the continuation and unfolding of the story was to produce some highly charged moments, such as Erich Mendelsohn's visit to the grain elevators in the harbor of Buffalo. The second *rappel* seems to have been far less galvanic in its effects, possibly because, in spite of its use of illustrations of factory buildings that were just as devoid of customary architectural airs and graces as were the elevators, it dealt with matters that were more literally as well as figuratively superficial—the use of regulating geometry in the design of facades:

To leave a mass intact in the splendor of its form in light, but, at the same time to appropriate its surface for needs that are utilitarian is to force oneself to discover in this unavoidable dividing up of the surface the accusing and generating lines of the form. In other words, an architectural structure is a house, a temple or a factory. The surface of the temple or the factory is in most cases a wall with holes for doors and windows: these holes are often the destruction of the form.[39]

The way in which the familiar form/function dichotomy is phrased here is unusual; it almost seems to echo Worringer's equally unusual function/form analysis of the aesthetic problems of an Egyptian pyramid:

A cubic shape was required by the practical purpose, namely the tomb chamber. On the other hand the construction was supposed to be a memorial, a memorial effective from a distance and solemnly impressive, that was to stand on a broad plain. A form had therefore to be found that was calculated to evoke most expressly the impression of material individuality and closed unity. To this, however, was opposed, for reasons set out earlier, the cubic framework required by the practical purpose.[40]

Le Corbusier is on a different track, however; his intention is not ultimately analytical but, rather, prescriptive. He prescribes a way of looking at the problem that is intended to assist the designer of buildings:

A wall with holes for doors and windows; these holes are often the destruction of form; they must be made the accentuation of form. If the essentials of architecture lie in spheres, cones and cylinders, the generating and accusing lines are on a basis of pure geometry. But this geometry terrifies the architect of today.[41]

The "architect of today" might not only plead terror, but confusion as well at this passage. The reference to "spheres, cones and cylinders" seems to have more to do with the forms whose masterly, cunning, and correct deployment in light had been the theme of the previous chapter than with the wide-glazed, concrete-framed factories that illustrate this second *rappel*. A page later, however, the connection is revealed as Le Corbusier gets back on course:

Everything tends to the restoration of simple masses; streets, factories, the large stores, all the problems which will present themselves tomorrow under a synthetic form and under general aspects that no other age has ever known. Surfaces pitted by holes in accordance with the necessities of their destined use, should borrow the generating and accusing lines of these simple forms. These accusing lines are in practice the chess-board or grill—American factories. But this geometry is a source of terror.

Not in pursuit of an architectural idea, but guided simply by the necessities of an imperative demand, the tendency of the engineers of today is towards the generating and accusing lines of masses; they show us the way and create plastic facts, clear and limpid, giving solace to our eyes and to the mind the pleasure of geometric forms.

Such are the factories, the reassuring first fruits of the new age. The engineers of today find themselves in accord with the principles that Bramante and Raphael had applied a long time ago.[42]

This last assertion serves to illustrate what has most significantly changed in the view of the Concrete Atlantis in the years between Gropius's first drawing attention to the American industrial buildings and Le Corbusier's return to them after the war. Whereas for Gropius they had been simply exemplars for a better modern industrial architecture, for Le Corbusier they had become—like the Tempietto of Bramante—exemplars for all architecture, forever, much as the book is entitled simply "Towards *an* Architecture" without any epithet or subsidiary clause to qualify the word "architecture." Le Corbusier here stands as more than a simple modernist; his claim is to speak for the architecture of all time.

Thus, what had started out as high-principled but modest proposals for the reform of one specialized branch of architecture—the design of better industrial buildings—has now become a presumptuous bid to possess the very soul of the Mother of the Arts or, at least, to remind architects what the soul of their art could be in its most purified state.

Almost as if he sensed how perilously high the argument had been pitched, Le Corbusier comes down to earth at the end of this second *rappel* with what must be the sauciest and most effective graphical *coup de théâtre* of his whole polemical career. When one turns the page to discover how the argument concludes, one finds simply a kind of postscript:

NB. Let us listen to the counsels of American engineers, but let us beware of American architects. For proof:[43]

and there follows a view of the neo-Baroque upper works of the Spreckles skyscraper in San Francisco, with all its reinforced concrete domes and pediments and cornices and columns!

Atlantis as Commonly Understood

Le Corbusier had advanced the argument to the point where American industrial structures exemplified at least two of the three great ruling principles of architecture—all architecture at all times. The version of these proposals that was commonly accepted and believed was probably a shade more modest. The argument was only likely to be noticed or believed by modernists like himself, after all. Those who were still inclined to put their faith in tradition and revived period styles would be disinclined to give much credence to this radical who claimed that "a house is a machine to live in" and that a Gothic cathedral was not very interesting. Given the inevitable defection of those who thought of themselves as traditionalists, the three *rappels* would be understood as being arguments about/for modern architecture alone—thus effectively thwarting Le Corbusier's most profound intentions, of course.

but, on the other hand, to appropriate its surface for needs which are often utilitarian, is to force oneself to discover in this unavoidable dividing up of the surface the *accusing* and

generating lines of the form. In other words, an architectural structure is a house, a temple or a factory. The surface of the temple or the factory is in most cases a wall with holes for doors and windows ; these holes are often the destruction of form ; they must be made an accentuation of form. If the

American factories and the Fagus-werk, first phase. (From *Towards a New Architecture*)

N.B. Let us listen to the counsels of American engineers. But let us beware of American architects. For proof :

The Spreckles Building, San Francisco, California, with Le Corbusier's comments. (From *Towards a New Architecture*)

Modernism and Americanism **229**

Even so, this still left his views a large constituency among European architects, who had been thoroughly prepared for them by the more restricted arguments Walter Gropius had advanced in "Die Entwicklung Moderner Industriebaukunst." Indeed, one must wonder if the credibility of Le Corbusier's arguments was not materially assisted by the fact that four of his most important illustrations had already been rendered familiar by the *Jahrbuch* article. For it should be emphasized (as if emphasis were needed!) that the ultimate conviction, credibility, or reassurance lay in the pictures, not the words, and such pictures continued to be discovered and printed throughout the twenties. Nearly all histories or apologias for modern architecture contain one or more views of grain elevators, in particular. Thus Walter Curt Behrendt's *Der Sieg des Neuen Baustils* of 1927 reproduces two of the *Jahrbuch* illustrations, and Bruno Taut's *Modern Architecture* (which may, in 1929, have been their first presentation to an English-reading audience outside Etchell's translation of *Vers une Architecture*) not only has two illustrations of familiar examples, but also extends the canon by including a view of Concrete Central in Buffalo, not previously seen in the architectural literature. Photographs by Erich Mendelsohn also helped extend the canon, not only through publication in his own works like *Amerika,* but through further reproduction in, for instance, Albert Morancé's *Architecture vivante* portfolios and even in Lewis Mumford's *Technics and Civilization,* where one of his pictures of a grain elevator is directly associated, for the first time, with the name of Worringer and his "suggestive essay on Egypt and America."[44]

The list could be extended to the point of tedium, so widespread and pervasive were these images. What is more to the point at this juncture is to establish how and why they achieved such penetration. Behrendt gave a clue in his nicely condensed version of what might be termed the official myth when he looked back on the period from the distance of a decade and the width of the Atlantic in his English-language text, *Modern Building:*

To do justice, it is necessary to say, and this will probably surprise the reader, that it was the example of America that gave the impulse to the German architects when they first tried to clarify the problem of structure. To be sure, this impulse did not originate in the skyscraper . . . but the simple structures of industrial building such as the grain elevators and big silos to be found in the great ports all over South America. These examples of modern engineering, designed for practical use only, and obviously without any decorative assistance from an architect, made a deep impression by their simple structure reduced to basic forms of geometry such as cubes and cylinders. They were conceived as patterns exemplifying once more the essence of the pure form of use, gaining its impressive effect from its bare structure.

The influence spreading from this pattern was soon apparent, and indeed was sometimes so strong as to lead to mere · imitation.[45]

Behrendt, however, may be a witness of unreliable memory, since the only example of such "mere imitation" that he produces is the design for the watertower and related structures at the municipal gasworks in Frankfurt-am-Main, whose cylindrical forms resemble those of American grain elevators only in being cylindrical but not in finish, detailing, or grouping. In any case, the date of the design is early 1911, which makes it extremely unlikely that its architect, Peter Behrens himself, could have known any relevant American examples. Nevertheless, Behrendt may be given general credence—even when misinformed, he was too unimaginative to have gravely distorted the record. The testimony of men with fundamentally ordinary minds can be of the greatest value, and one of the most valuable of such witnesses has become available in English only recently: the Russian architect Moisei Ginzburg (1892–1946).

The fact that he was Russian might suggest that he was not culturally close enough to be relevant to the present argument; but even if the content of his writings did not make the matter perfectly clear, the Russian architects of the revolutionary generation were probably more closely in touch with world developments in their art than any cohort of Russians before or since, and their contributions, in ideas, designs, and persons, to the worldwide movement to modernize architecture are a matter of record. Furthermore, in the early days of the Soviet regime the technological modernization of Russia was frequently seen in terms of the straightforward imitation of America or even the direct importation of American technology and expertise, such as in the commission to Ford and Albert Kahn to set up tractor plants between 1929 and 1932. Yet these specific developments came after Ginzburg's book; in his admiration for the Concrete Atlantis, he was ahead of the official game.

Ginzburg's early writings are intelligent, well informed, and versed in world developments—which should hardly be surprising since he studied at the Ecole des Beaux-Arts in Paris, the Accademia di Belli Arti in Milan, and the Polytechnic in Riga, one of the great nurseries of Russian architectural talent before the Revolution as well as one of the most cosmopolitan of Russian schools. His built work is always extremely competent, without ever approximating genius, and his thinking seems to match. A complete professional, he may properly stand as an *architecte moyen sensuel* of the modern persuasion.

He knew the work of Wölfflin, Worringer, and Spengler, so he is clearly part of the cultural milieu in which American industrial structures were domesticated into European architecture. His book *Stil'i epokha* (*Style and Epoch*) of 1924 has been described as seminal, which it may well have been in Russia; but he was not much ahead of the architectural game as far as the rest of Europe was concerned, except for the one thing that has always assured him a place in the esteem of a certain faction of architectural historians: his invention of the "Stroikom" (split-level, crossover central corridor) section for apartment blocks, later apparently imitated by Wells Coates in England and, more consequentially, by Le Corbusier in the Unité d'Habitation at Marseille.

This last might almost be seen as the reclamation of an old debt by Le Corbusier, since there seems to be good evidence that *Stil'i epokha* is based, in part at least, on a reading of the earlier articles that were to form part of *Vers une Architecture,* including the three *rappels.* But what is most interesting in this connection is that when Ginzburg illustrates a grain elevator, it is not one of the Gropius-Corbusier set that were to become canonical images. His illustrations are strictly his own, and throughout the book they strike a note of independent originality, even when they illustrate mechanistic themes that were becoming commonplace, such as aircraft, ships, bridges, cooling towers, and the like. His factories and aircraft are Italian (Ansaldo, Fiat, Caproni), his locomotives and earth-moving equipment are German (Kraus). His grain elevators are all in Buffalo, but even when they are examples that appear in other literature (Washburn-Crosby, Kellog), they are seen in unfamiliar views, while one, the Electric, is unknown in the rest of the modernist literature. If his illustrations are unfamiliar, however, his arguments are quite the opposite.

As the title suggests, the book employs the familiar cyclical schema of the rise and decline of styles and classifies them into the customary complementary pairings: Classic/Gothic, Renaissance/Baroque, and so on. If we can discern the hand of Wölfflin in this, we can also discern the unmistakably Spenglerian proposition that the older styles are all exhausted, as is the established European culture that produced them. To counter this, Ginzburg calls for new beginnings, for "barbarian invasions"; otherwise

cultures would fall into a state of perpetual old age and helpless atrophy lasting for ever, since it is impossible to chew perpetually on the same old food. What is needed, at all costs, is the daring blood of barbarians who do not know what they are creating.[46]

These barbarians, as we see in the rest of the book, might well be the kind of noble savages of the modern technological world whom we have encountered already. But they are now given another reassuring root in the classicizing past. In this version Leon Battista Alberti's well-known proposition (from the *De Re Aedificatoria*) that a building is beautiful when nothing can be added and nothing taken away without spoiling the whole, is adduced and then made an analogue to the modern machine, which has only, and exactly, the parts needed to perform its designed function. Ginzburg's barbarians, like the noble savages of engineering in Le Corbusier, will be some kind of primitive classicists.

And whatever their ideological roots, it is from America that Ginzburg, like everyone else, sees these new barbarians coming:

If Europe, with its vast size, presents a picture of complete decline, America, primarily the United States of North America, offers a more instructive view.

A new national power that has not yet had the time to accumulate its own traditions and artistic experience quite naturally turns to Europe for assistance; Europe, true to the stodgy ideals of its classical system, begins transporting its products across the ocean. However, the life of North America as a vital new power cannot, despite its own wishes, proceed along a course well trodden by other cultures. An American tempo of life is emerging, utterly different from that of Europe—businesslike, dynamic, sober, mechanized, devoid of any Romanticism. . . . Nevertheless, wishing to be "as good as" Europe, America continues to import European aesthetics and romanticism as though they were commodities that had stood the test of time and been "patented" as it were. Thus there emerges a single aspect of America: a horrifying mechanical mixture of new, organic, purely American elements with the superficial envelopes of an outlived classical system "made in Europe." . . .

Yet at the same time, in those instances when the American genius permitted itself the luxury of doing without Europe's help, when the crude and sober but nonetheless potentially vigorous spirit of the new pioneers manifested itself, brilliant structures teeming with unexpected poignancy and force were created spontaneously in an absolutely organic manner. I have in mind the industrial structures of America, and we shall have more to say about them later.[47]

Perhaps because this is so largely derivative, as well as informed and intelligent, it gives as clear and compact a picture as we are likely to get of the modern architect's America, a bright prospect of the Concrete Atlantis far across the sea and thus ultimately beyond the reach of an old and decrepit Europe. And it is a prospect that will inevitably become true even of rural Russia:

No matter what our predilections, life sooner or later will demand that we provide even the countryside with electric power, supply it with a multitude of various machines, dot its quiet plains with tractors, and enliven its horizons with elevators.[48]

The last illustration to the penultimate chapter of *Stil'i epokha* is of the Kellog elevator in Buffalo, and on the same page one finds:

In the industrial structures of the last decade in the largest cities of Europe and America we see already realized not only the foundations of a modern aesthetic, but even the individual elements of architecture, systems of supports, joints, spans, openings, terminations, flashes of compositional schemes and flashes of new forms, which can already be transferred to domestic architecture, can already serve as the concrete and profoundly practical material that will be able to help the architect find a true course for creative work and help transform the language of abstract aesthetics into a precise lexikon of architecture. Such is the role of industrial architecture.[49]

Whether one interprets this as high art or low cunning, as a call for a new kind of "language of architecture" or merely the discovery of a handy copybook of modern details for desperate architects suffering from "designers' block," it still sees the uses of America in rather a different frame of reference from anything that had been proposed before. Ginzburg is bringing the argument nearer to the drawing boards of practicing architects in search of ways to an immediately buildable future:

It is from industrial architecture rather than from anywhere else that we can expect realistic indications concerning how and in what way these paths can be found. What we are talking about here is adding to the existing landscape of modernity—the machine, the engineering and industrial structures— the latest link in the architectural chain: residential and public buildings equal to these structures.[50]

Ginzburg's last chapter, and even the selection of illustrations of works by his Russian contemporaries at the end of the book, is also introduced by otherwise unexplained images of elevators in Buffalo. In thus persistently offering these American industrial structures as practical exemplars for comparison, if not exact emulation, he goes well beyond anything proposed by Gropius or Le Corbusier. He seems to be in the process of reducing the Concrete Atlantis from the heights of visionary utopianism to something much nearer to what most average architects could understand and believed they needed: a school of form.

In the end, it was to be a school not generally followed. Europe and Soviet Russia would find their way into a buildable modern future without directly copying American industrial buildings form for form, though much may have been learned in less literal terms. However, there is one spectacular exception to this blanket rule, a deliberate emulation of the forms and scale, the structure and processes, of American industry. It was a building that Ginzburg illustrated in *Stil'i epokha,* and it is practically the only example of modern industrial building that he seems to have in common with Le Corbusier and everyone else in the modern movement. Where Ginzburg differs from the rest of the movement, however, is that he was not photographed on that building's roof, like any other self-conscious modernist worthy of the name, from Gabriele d'Annunzio to F. T. Marinetti and beyond. This building that was to become Europe's own talismanic American building and a very touchstone of modernity was the Fiat automobile plant at Lingotto, in the inner suburbs of Turin, Italy.

Fiat-Lingotto and the Vision of a Timeless New Order

The Fiat factory at Turin–Lingotto was always intended to be what it now appears to be: a factory in the American style. Its resemblances to the kind of regular Daylight factory discussed earlier in this book are as striking in small details as they are in its general structure or its large-scale composition; indeed, the very magnitude by which it exceeds in size any of the Fiat company's previous installations is part of its consciously American intentions—to rationalize production and to achieve "the economies of scale." One could perhaps argue that there is no really radical break between Lingotto and what Fiat had built before by drawing an analogy with what had been done by Ford in Detroit from the time of the Picquette Street plant through the Old Shop at Highland Park to the New Shop and beyond. These events had paced the development of the Fiat plants at a lead time of approximately ten years and represent an equivalent progression from early buildings that were modest in scale and conventional in construction to concrete behemoths that were neither modest nor conventional in design.

Fiat's building history certainly begins in modest ways. The oldest surviving plant (1898) on the Corso Dante in Turin, for instance, has a form of brick-pier construction behind the present stucco, as does the slightly later installation for the manufacture of *Motori Grandi* on the via Cuneo and via Dominiani; and there is good evidence in the numerous early industrial buildings that survive in Turin that there was a well-established brick-building tradition in that city for factories and warehouses. On the other hand, there is nothing to be seen, nothing known in the documentation, to suggest that there was ever a local equivalent of Albert Kahn, no experimental, innovative structure like Packard 10, to bridge the gap between the older tradition and the stunningly new type of factory that is represented by Lingotto.

What came out of that locally unprecedented leap in scale, construction, and production technology was a building that is frequently compared to Ford's Old Shop at Highland Park and is generally understood in Turin to have been meant to invite such comparison by Giovanni Agnelli, Fiat's boss. The occasion for this drastic change in operating style was the decision of the company to go over to a Ford style of mass-production, though the layout of the production process adopted at Lingotto would have struck most of Ford's higher management as illogical and eccentric, at the very least. Design work in the new plant appears to have begun in 1914, under the direction of the *ingegnerone* ("super-engineer,"

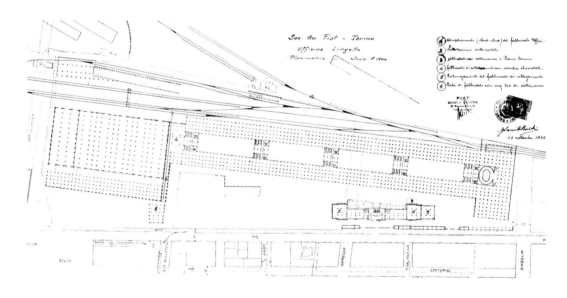

Fiat-Lingotto, Turin, Italy, by Giacomo Matté-Trucco et al., 1914–1926. (Photo courtesy of Fiat Archives, Turin)

Fiat-Lingotto, plan. (Courtesy, City Building Archives of Turin)

more or less) Giacomo Matté-Trucco, Fiat's Director of Production. The building made Matté-Trucco famous, but as Cesare de'Seta has observed, he then "would vanish completely from the Italian architectural scene."[51] It is clear that Matté-Trucco was not the architect of the building in any normal sense of the word, though his, and Agnelli's, are the only signatures on any drawings I have seen. On the company's payroll at that time was Vittorio Bonadé Bottino, a Torinese civil engineer specializing in concrete work who was presumably connected with the design of the works; but the visual evidence, inside and out, seems almost overwhelmingly to indicate the presence of American designers or consultants on the team.[52]

Site work began in 1916, and the building campaign lasted for the whole of the next decade.[53] The main body of the works, effectively in place by 1920, is a single building, five stories high and composed of two parallel blocks over five hundred meters long, linked by three cross-blocks. The plan is thus unlike either Ford's Old Shop, which is four stories in a single block without light wells but is even longer, or the New Shop, which is higher than Lingotto but much more nearly square in plan. And where the New Shop is penetrated by the high aisles through which the railroad tracks can pass, at Fiat the railroad sidings are outside the building and come up to it at an angle. What Fiat-Lingotto seems most like as a production building is Ransome's United Shoe Machinery plant, especially in its cross-blocks and light wells; and by 1920 it would have looked equally antiquated to American eyes. Ford, to take the obvious comparison, was transferring production to the enormous single-story, steel-framed facilities at remotely suburban River Rouge—a totally different conception of industrial building and organization.

It is very strange indeed to experience the antiquated Americanism of Lingotto at first hand. In 1984 I walked through its deserted production floors and felt that I must have been transported to some legendary *lontane Americhe,* so similar were nearly all the details and dimensions. Here were square concrete columns approximating the standard fourteen-inch sections with chamfered edges that could be

Fiat, *Motori Grandi,* Turin, 1900—5.
(Photo, author)

Fiat-Lingotto, facade to via Nizza.
(Photo, author)

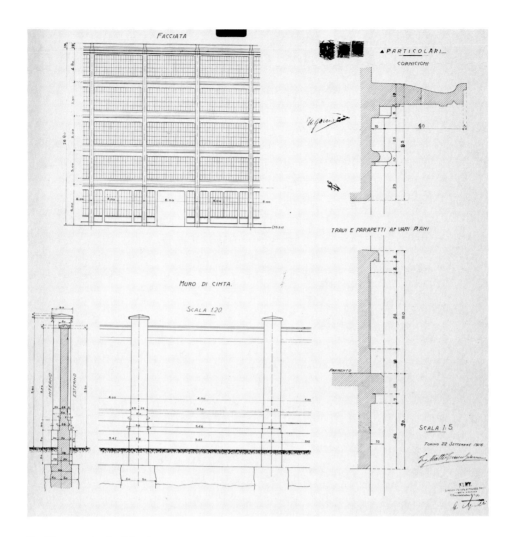

Fiat-Lingotto, details of facade.
(Courtesy City Building Archives of
Turin)

seen anywhere in the industrial northeast. The column spacing at six meters was almost exactly to American standards, too; and the outward view was through steel industrial sash that looked suspiciously like the standard Crittall sash that America had imported from England in the earliest years of the present century. I could have been back in Buffalo, but for the fact that the surviving graffiti and pin-ups were unmistakably Italian, and but for one detail that would be hard to parallel in common American factory construction—the perforation of the horizontal beams with regular rectangular holes to accept the passage of piping and electrical conduitry. It was a strangely disturbing and moving experience for me, a kind of historian's homecoming for one partially Americanized European whose prime subject of study has been the International Style.

However, it is not this conspicuous Americanism, fundamental to the whole conception and construction of the building, that has fixed Lingotto so firmly in the history of modern architecture—and of modern Italy, too. The cause of that unique place of esteem is the crowning glory of the whole project: the high-speed test track on the roof, which is something that most (perhaps all) American factory builders would have regarded as a piece of economic folly as grotesque, in its vaster way, as the ostentatiously "missing" columns at the glazed corners of the Faguswerk. Yet, in its folly, the Fiat roof track is magnificent, and European, for at this level the detailing has a slight flavor of Auguste Perret about it.

One ascends nowadays to the rooftop track by means of the handsome helical concrete ramps at either end of the track, ramps that were to become almost as famous as the track itself and to be as widely illustrated, especially in the 1930s. They were not part of the original concept and were added to the design as part of a more radical reconsideration of internal movement within the plant that would enable small tractors to pull trains of hand trucks from one floor to another on demand, without having to wait for elevator space. There are other signs, too, that the original concept was found wanting in efficiency: the 1924 additions at the north end of the block also include a three-bay limb at the back, extending over railroad sidings which pass through it in a four-story unloading craneway that appears to be directly descended from the tall aisles in Ford's New Shop at Highland Park.

Wherever one ascends, however, the ramps deliver the rolling vehicle into a cramped and awkward space under the shadow behind one of the banked turns that remain an essential part of the image of the building. Squeezed between the flank of the banking and the parapet on the edge of the building, one emerges suddenly on to the track, which extends half a kilometer to where the other banking rises and turns to the left to deliver the vehicle to the return straight of the track. To see it for the first time, as I did, through the windscreen of a moving car is a nerve-tingling experience. One is entering one of the sacred places of European modernism, sanctified and certified by the photographically documented presence of practically every European Futurist, modernist, or other progressive spirit of note throughout the twenties and early thirties. And the shock of recognition is reinforced by the fact that it still looks exactly as it did in those historic photographs.

The reason for this eccentric location of the track—apart from a strain of Futurist mania appropriate to the time and place of the inception of the design—is integral to Matté-Trucco's concept of the organization of the production process to which it is the functional, as well as symbolic, crown. Contrary to the American tradition to gravity-flow processes (invented by Oliver Evans for his flour mill and confirmed by Ford at Highland Park), where materials and components enter the plant at the top and exit as finished products at the bottom, the work flow at Lingotto is from the bottom upward. Parts and materials enter the plant at ground level and move to the final assembly lines on the top floor. From there the "neo-nato" would emerge into Turin's smoggy sunshine on the roof, there to prove itself on the test track before finally returning to ground level in the parking yards between the plant and the via Nizza.

One cannot help but wonder what kind of "functionalism" the whole project for a rooftop test track was supposed to embody. Notoriously, serious high-speed testing was done on the via Nizza itself (usually in the very early morning to avoid the attentions of the police!). Any American manufacturer building a plant on a "green field" site would have laid out a test track, if needed, on an adjacent piece of land, not on the roof of the plant. In the end Fiat had to abandon the rooftop track for all serious purposes; the reason usually given is that the vibration of vehicles thundering round the track above was threatening the integrity of the structure by literally shaking it to pieces. I could see little evidence of this during my visit, but I did discover a more convincing reason for discontinuing its use—it is not to be taken seriously as a *high-speed* test track, whatever may have been intended and was believed, and it requires only half a lap of driving to see why this should be the case.

The bends at either end are disproportionately sharp, though they cannot be otherwise, given the width of the building. The super-elevation of the bankings is steep—about 27 degrees—and they are of the approved parabolic section, correctly laid out and beautifully surfaced in granite setts, installed diamond-wise to accommodate the three-dimensional curvature. But the transitions between the flat straights and the banked bends are almost incredibly bad, inexcusably so at this date, since the geometrical theory of long, curving transitions had been reduced to available "cookbook" procedures by them, after the building of innumerable banked circuits for both automobile and bicycle racing on both sides of the Atlantic.[54] Yet Lingotto's transitions, by an inelegantly short, twisted ramp—dictated, as one can clearly see by looking up at the ceiling of the top floor, by the bay-widths and structural dispositions of the building—are so sudden that even a modern car with sophisticated suspension and superior tire grip is in body-rolling, tire-squealing difficulties above a mere 60 kph.

What skills must have been demanded of test-drivers in the twenties can hardly be imagined now. With their narrow tires and cart-type springing, many Fiat models were never-

Fiat-Lingotto, interior of a work
floor. (Photo, Claudio Dapra)

theless already capable of 70 kph. even before Lingotto was completed; and the mass-produced cars of the late twenties, at the beginning of the period of the factory's greatest fame, were generally capable of better than 80 kph. The track could therefore have been used less for absolute high-speed testing than for checking that all moving parts did really move, controls were in order, and electrical connections satisfactorily made—something that many manufacturers can effectively accomplish by simply driving the product from the end of the production line to the parking lot.

Must Europe's most acclaimed invention in industrial architecture be accounted a failure then, even if a heroic failure? It does appear possible that from the point of view of production efficiency, of the rationality of capitalist profit, Lingotto was only a modest success, and was eventually replaced as the company's main facility by their own new shop at Mirafiore. As a symbol of the modernization of Italy, however, it was a triumph, acclaimed by Marinetti as *La prima invenzione costruttiva futurista*[53] ("the prime invention of Futurist construction"), and its value to the civic life of Turin cannot be counted in mere money. As Antonello Negri said of it, Lingotto is "a presence in the city, a standing witness to the period."

Yet immediately after this encomium to its mighty presence, Negri utters the startling phrase: "With Lingotto, the period of industrial archaeology closes."[56]

Admittedly he was writing about the fairly narrow topic of industrial archaeology in Lombardy alone, but even so the phrase is striking. By inverting common interpretations and locating Lingotto at the end of archaeology rather than at the beginning of the modernist future, Negri's words have an appropriate and elegiac ring. The plant is moving to visit, not only in the way that the abandoned fabrics of the Gritty Cities of the American northeast are moving, as witnesses of a lost enterprise, but because this particular enterprise was so special and European in its objectives, its industrial and cultural aspirations, that it is a kind of testament to a lost future.

As a stylistic choice, its design seems already a vision of an exotic past, as surely as if it had been built in some Pharaonic or Doric mode. If one sees it simply as a derivative and provincial version of a manner of building whose metropolitan heartland was elsewhere, however, one must yet recognize that the vision of that distant heartland was still optimistic, futuristic, and utopian; and the choice of an American model for that envisioned future is a mark of what had changed, and how profoundly, not only in industrial architecture, but in the modernist view of architecture at large. Because it is the most literal-minded realization of the European dream of the Concrete Atlantis, it is also the most poignant.

The poignancy of Lingotto is increased by an extraordinary accolade—perhaps the most remarkable piece of writing ever devoted to an industrial structure—it received in 1927 from Edoardo Persico, generally regarded as the most intelligent and sensitive of all the younger Italian designers who were to perish in the *difficoltà politiche* of the Fascist epoch. Neapolitan in origin, literary in his early interests, Persico is reputed to have been a member of Mussolini's first embassy to Soviet Russia,[57] which could well be true, though this part of his life is "officially" a blank. When he returned to Turin, he appears to have run into his first political difficulties and spent some time in prison. He later surfaced in Milan, where he was a highly visible member of the art and design community until his death (of sheer loneliness, it is said) in 1936. When he wrote of Lingotto, he spoke from personal experience; not only had he worked in the plant in his Torinese years, but he also had a sharp sense of the part that Americanism had played in the modernism (and modernization) of the Italian north:

Let us put ourselves a long way back, into 1914; Sant'Elia—
"We no longer feel ourselves to be men of the cathedrals and ancient moot halls, but of the great hotels, railroad stations, giant streets, colossal harbors, covered markets, glittering arcades, grid-iron planning and salutary slum clearances." Have our architects, or our polemicists, yet considered how large a part an obsession with American culture must have played in

Fiat-Lingotto, section at spiral ramp.
(Courtesy City Building Archives of
Turin)

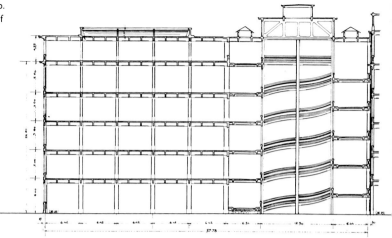

this manifesto. . . . In 1914, in Milan, Sant'Elia could in no way avoid the cosmopolitan fevers of the city, and dreamed of New York.[58]

That was written later. In 1927 he wrote of Lingotto, not as part of any American dream (he may not even have known of Agnelli's intentions), but on the basis of its daily presence as the landscape of his working life; as a concrete and monumental object large enough, complex enough, yet logical enough to engage his imagination and his moral and religious sensibilities and to set him meditating on the necessary laws of industry, architecture, man, and the universe. It was his first writing about any building and may stand here as the last argument of this book, as a provisional revelation of what that "ultimate metaphysic of form" might be, the secret order of that Concrete Atlantis beyond the Western ocean.[59]

At the end of a suburban street, among the last industries and the scaffoldings for the newest houses, the Fiat factory stands up in the logic of its architecture. A construction of incomparably clear forms, whose simplicity of aspect proclaims the principles of order. This plant seems to exist in itself, like a moral concept, a model of the structure of the Law. And in this aspect it has concentrated the labor of centuries, as if the strength of infinite generations had finally produced a norm of economy, from which is born an impression of the beauty of the identity of

Fiat-Lingotto, southern ramp.
(Photo, Claudio Dapra)

a thing with its function. A work of intelligence that has found the link between grace and necessity by pure deduction. This accomplished grandeur is like an image of Man and of his concerns. In its simple appearance, where combinations of curves and straight lines have fashioned a moment of Eternity, there is manifested a human quest that has resolved its uncertainties in obedience to the Law. As with the style of the cathedrals, this factory has concluded its search for the divine at a moment of history. It is like a harbor, with an immense arsenal and two square towers. From the top, where cars run as it were around the battlements, the horizon evokes the presence of sails and the beginnings of a navigation out into the world. The machines parked in the yards below seem like moored vessels that will set forth tomorrow. . . .

Atop the building, the test track is like a king's crown, and just as a crown symbolizes some essential and dominating idea, so here the car and its speed are celebrated in a form that presides over the work of the factory below, not only in terms of utility, but also following a secret standard that governs the ends of things. A mysterious logic of harmony—which the architect has obeyed intuitively as a sign of authority—has elevated this test track to the pinnacle of a work of man: much as the authority of the crown on the brow of a king transcends the

*merely human face below and weighs upon it with the force of
a dominant rule. In its own structure, the track is a concrete
image of speed. It expresses the idea of the car in a clear concept: nothing may stand still here. From the crests of the
parabolas that define the curves there derives an ideal line that
crosses the grids to regain its origin, where it resumes the rise
and fall, to infinity. On this track nothing can deny the car without developing a different line, creating an alternative order and
abolishing the Laws. As if to the principle of authority, everything refers itself to this uplifted place, and to it ascend the
working elements as they are integrated into their machines.
Like individuals, the components gather together from everywhere, and where the crown sits they are united and combine in
a single fact and a single idea, which is unity. On the roof of
Fiat, as in a speck of consciousness hovering over the abyss of
liberty, Man may scrutinize the Laws. On this track, elevated as
it were above every country, the Prince of Denmark might pace,
as in his castle of Elsinore, and elevated above time as well,
interrogate his destiny.*

*Two routes lead up to this place of inward concentration and
uphold it as a spiritual fact. Only the track is free beneath the
heavens and before God. The means by which the workers can
reach it are concealed within the factory like a perpetual, buried
aspiration. The meaning of these two rising spirals is obedience:
to set foot upon them means to understand the secret motive of
discipline that connects every part of the works to its summit,
that is, to the supreme end of everything. The ramps seem to
grow downward from above, upward from below, according to
natural reason. They are not sustained by massive beams, no
mechanical construction is to be seen; only a harmony, and a
law, that pervades them by virtue of a principle that seems
cosubstantial with their material. At the appointed place de-
creed by the foresight of the order, the workshops obey their
prescribed exercise, and by this route the varied works are
melded into a single form of obedience, right up to the test
track. These spirals are indeed a road to human liberty, where
everything is elaborated in the individual, fused into the mass*

and is integrated into a unity. The same restless rotation is in these spiral ramps, and in the life that has fashioned them in its own image.

At morning, dominated by the stare of these great glass eyes that have the impassivity of justice, the workers wait under the hollow, cyclopean walls. They do not speak, they do not move as they would in other human assemblies; they wait. All things are already in order, nothing can be changed, everything obeys an order which is not the expression of human will, but of a wisdom submissive to the Laws. They await the Laws. They are a people still confused, without order, an image of humanity without rules. These seem to be the principles of history and all things possible: order and disorder, sin and obedience. They have more need of order than of bread. In the forecourt they look like the crowds at ancient theaters; the high wall reinforces the impression, almost like the Colosseum. As in some ancient play, these people seem to await a catastrophe; that is, what follows the strophe, which was the word of God, the command of Justice. Order in every form prevails always in this scene, where everything must obey the Laws. Revolution—in some yet distant day—has not yet broken the circle of command, everyone has returned to his function, his post, as yesterday and tomorrow. When the closing hooter blows, they all come forth again like vast battalions that follow a banner; they are led by an invisible banner on which are written inexorable words that men may forget at times, but which the will of God has written on the conscience of the people, the true flock of the Law. An ancient order of obedience.

At night, seen from the train, it shines with the light of its lamps and the reflections of the forges; it looks like an enormous castle where all the light of the world is stored, a rock of fire tunneled by a million gnomes. . . .

And if it should happen that you are passing under its walls as evening falls and the soul is weighed down with the insuperable melancholy of the Nordic twilight, perhaps you will see the broad shades of the lamps that are still lit as so many medusas floating in an immense aquarium. . . . And you will salute Fiat as an undeniable sign placed in your way to teach you to subdue your egoism and to live in good order.

Notes

Introduction

1.
Steinbeck, *Cannery Row* (Penguin edition), 1973, pp. 143–144.

2.
The structure has now been removed and the site cleared to accommodate road realignments in connection with the new Monterey Aquarium.

3.
Etlin, "Le Corbusier, Choisy and the Architectural Promenade," paper delivered at the annual conference of the Society of Architectural Historians, Pittsburgh, PA, April 1985.

4.
Venturi, Scott-Brown, and Izenour, *Learning from Las Vegas*, 1972, pp. 92–93.

5.
Walter Gropius, "Die Entwicklung Moderner Industriebaukunst." English translation as "The Development of Modern Industrial Architecture," in Benton, Benton, and Sharp, *Form and Function*, 1975, pp. 53–54.

6.
Le Corbusier, *Vers une Architecture.* English translation by Frederick Etchells, *Towards a New Architecture*, 1927, p. 33.

7.
Mendelsohn, *Letters of an Architect*, edited by Oscar Beyer, 1967, p. 69.

8.
Le Corbusier, p. 33.

9.
"The New Atlantis," in *Essays and New Atlantis*, edited by George S. Haight, 1942, p. 264.

10.
Le Corbusier, p. 33.

11.
Gropius, pp. 53–54.

12.
See, for instance, the various papers from "Das Andere" anthologized by Loos himself in *Trotzdem*, 1931, pp. 11–50.

13.
Jahrbuch des Deutschen Werkbundes, 1913, "Die Kunst in Industrie und Handel"; the insert of illustrations follows p. 16.

14.
Letter in the Archive Le Corbusier, Paris, reported to me by Jacques Paul and Joyce Lowman.

15.
Behrendt, *Der Sieg des Neuen Baustils*, 1927, p. 22.

16.
Scully, *American Architecture and Urbanism*, 1969, p. 123. This illustration and its caption neatly encapsulate the passage of these images into the mythology of modern architecture and their absorption into American

architectural culture. Scully, needing only to make a general point about American grain elevators, which he could have illustrated by sending out a student with a camera, nevertheless uses one of the Gropius images, as altered by Le Corbusier, and then captions it as being in Buffalo, whereas it still stood, at that time, in Montreal!

17.
Le Corbusier, p. 33.

18.
Cahiers d'Art 5, 1926, p. 114.

19.
For a judicious account of the German debates on the flat roof, see: Pommer, "The Flat Roof," *Art Journal* 40:2 (Summer 1983): 155–169.

Chapter 1

1.
Le Corbusier, *Towards a New Architecture*, 1927, pp. 37–41.

2.
Such trade literature from two generations of the Ransome family seems to be distributed randomly through libraries on both sides of the Atlantic. A complete checklist would be of the greatest value to historical studies.

3.
Condit, *American Building Art*, 1968, p. 172. Port Costa was called "Wheatport" in its early days, and the date given for the present structure is 1887, within a year of that given by Condit, though he describes the structure as a flour mill. The uncertainty of this attribution stems largely from the fact that Condit has offered no reference for the source of his discussion of "Wheatport" and is increased by the fact that the illustration which he appears to be offering as the floor system at "Wheatport" (illustration 61a) is identified by Ransome (*Reinforced Concrete Buildings*, p. 7) as that of the Pacific Coast Borax Company's factory extension at Alameda, California.

4.
Giedion, *Space, Time and Architecture*, 5th ed., 1967, p. 357.

5.
American Architect and Building News XCIX: 1851 (June 14, 1911): 214.

6.
Engineering News XL (July 7, 1898): 15.

7.
Such footnotes all seem to derive from "Frame of Steel" by Leonard K. Eaton, *Architectural Review* 126 (November 1959): 189–190.

8.
American Architect and Building News, p. 213.

9.
Atlas Portland Cement Co., *Reinforced Concrete in Factory Construction*, 1907, p. 237.

10.
As reported to me by the plant manager.

11.
Ransome and Saurbrey, *Reinforced Concrete Buildings*, 1912, p. 10.

12.
Ibid., pp. 12–13, 162–170.

13.
The original project is illustrated in *The Legacy of Albert Kahn*, 1970, p. 40.

14.
Hitchcock, catalogue introduction, 1940; reprinted in Banham, et al., *Buffalo Architecture, A Guide*, 1981, p. 35.

15.
Now in the possession of John Quinan of Buffalo, NY.

16.
Hildebrand, *Designing for Industry: The Architecture of Albert Kahn*, 1974, p. 45.

17.
See especially, Ellery, *Permanency in Building Construction*, vol. 2, 1913.

Chapter 2

1.
Johnson's early work on steel-bin elevators as well as his pioneering brick elevator in Buffalo, NY, are noted and illustrated in Ransome and Saurbrey, *Reinforced Concrete Build-*

ings, p. 29, and extensively discussed in "Fireproof Grain-storage Buildings," *The Brick Builder* 11 (November 1902): 232–236, a fundamental source for his son's work on tile bins as well.

2.
Engineering News XLVI (August 1, 1901): 210.

3.
Nicholas Westbrook (ed.), *A Guide to the Industrial Archaeology of the Twin Cities*, 1983, p. 68.

4.
Gropius, "Die Entwicklung Moderner Industriebaukunst," in Benton, Benton, and Sharp, *Form and Function*, 1975, p. 56.

5.
Kennedy, "Fireproof Grain Elevators in North America," *Engineering News* XLVI (July 18, 1901): 42.

6.
The Brick Builder, pp. 232–236.

7.
Ibid.

8.
They spread farther afield than that, however, and thus—accidentally, perhaps—acquire a special importance for this study. The elevator identified by Gropius in his *Jahrbuch* article as "Getreidesilo Bunge y Born Buenos Aires"—and which Le Corbusier not only wrongly captioned as "Canadian," but also "censored" or "modernized" by having its numerous pediments whited out before publication—can be identified from earlier publications as "The largest Grain-Elevator in Argentina. It is built of brick [sic] and is the property of the Cia de Molinas y Elevadores del Rio de la Plata, Buenos Aires." (Overmire, "Modern Fireproof Grain Elevators," *The Northwestern Miller* 56: 21 (November 25, 1903): 1156).

9.
Gropius, "Die Entwicklung," p. 56.

10.
Worringer, *Egyptian Art* (English edition), 1928, p. X.

11.
Westbrook, p. 68.

12.
Heffelfinger, "Experiment in Concrete," in *Minnesota History* (March 1960): 14–20. My attention was drawn to this and other invaluable Minnesota references by Nicholas Westbrook, to whom I am extremely grateful.

13.
See *Engineering News* XLIV (December 27, 1900): 438, and also XLIX (May 7, 1903): 396.

14.
Engineering News XLIV, p. 438.

15.
Westbrook, p. 68.

16.
Mendelsohn, *Amerika: Bilderbuch eines Architekten*, 1926, p. 37.

17.
Building permits in the "vault" of Buffalo City Hall (searched out and indexed for me by Donald Theurer); *Buffalo of Today*, 1906–7, p. 33; *The Industrial Empire of Niagara*, 1918–1919, p. 41, etc.

18.
Le Corbusier, *Towards a New Architecture*, 1927, p. 32.

19.
Severance (ed.), *The Picture Book of Earlier Buffalo*, 1912, p. 42; *Buffalo of Today*, 1906–7, p. 9; *The Industrial Empire of Niagara*, 1918–1919, pp. 15, 39, etc.

20.
Moholy-Nagy, *Von Material zu Architektur*, 1929, p. 231.

21.
Prokter and Matuzaski, *Gritty Cities*, 1978, p. 14.

22.
Ozenfant, *Foundations of Modern Art.* English translation by John Rodker, augmented American edition, 1952, p. 155.

Chapter 3

1.
Benevolo, *History of Modern Architecture.* English translation, 1971, vol. 1, p. 387.

2.
Weber, *Walter Gropius und das Fagus-werk*, 1961, forms the main source for the entire narrative of the building of Fagus which follows.

3.
See the example at Wurms, completed 1908, illustrated in Müller-Wülckow, *Bauten der Arbeit und des Werkehrs*, 1929, p. 60.

4.
Giedion, *Walter Gropius Work and Teamwork*, 1954, p. 22.

5.
See Campbell, *The German Werkbund*, 1978, pp. 59–60, 65–66.

6.
Weber, p. 22. All the citations from the Folkwang lecture given here are translated by the author from the abbreviated version of this text given by Weber, but have subsequently been revised in light of the full text printed by Karin Wilhelm in *Walter Gropius, Industriearchitekt*, 1983, pp. 116–120.

7.
Worringer, *Egyptian Art* (English edition), 1928, p. X and plate 22.

8.
Weber, p. 27.

9.
Ibid., pp. 27–28.

10.
See "Clean, Well-lighted Places" in Chapter 1.

11.
Gropius, "Die Entwicklung Moderner Industriebaukunst," in Benton, Benton, and Sharp, *Form and Function*, 1975, p. 53.

12.
Ibid.

13.
Ibid., p. 54.

14.
Ibid.

15.
Ibid., pp. 54–55.

16.
Frank Lloyd Wright: Ausgeführten Bauten und Skizzen, 1910, and *Frank Lloyd Wright: Ausgeführten Bauten*, 1911.

17.
See "Architektur" in Loos, *Trotzdem*, 1931, p. 95ff.

18.
Wilhelm, *Walter Gropius, Industriearchitekt*, pp. 35–36.

19.
"Engineers are our Hellenes . . . from them we receive our culture." Loos, *Ins Leere gesprochen*, 1932, p. 58.

20.
Marinetti, *Le Futurisme*, 1912, p. 75.

21.
Worringer, *Abstraktion und Einfühlung*. English translation by Michael Bullock, 1953, p. 17.

22.
Ibid., p. 42.

23.
Ibid.

24.
Ibid., p. 90.

25.
Marling, "My Egypt; the irony of an American Dream," *Winterthur Portfolio* 15: 1 (Spring 1980): 25–37. Her paper is not otherwise of much help to the present study, in spite of its wide-ranging erudition. Thus she claims that Le Corbusier introduces *Vers une Architecture* with eight "glossy" pictures of grain elevators and compares them to Egyptian pyramids and temples, which may be literally true, but not very instructive since he equally compares them to the Parthenon, the Colosseum, Hardrian's Villa, the Pantheon, the Pont du Gard, Santa Sophia, etc. In a footnote she speculates whether Charles Demuth could just have had time to read Worringer's *Egyptian Art* in the original German before titling the picture, but makes no mention at all of Gropius, whose article had appeared over a decade before work on the painting commenced.

26.
Worringer, *Abstraktion*, p. 18.

27.
Müller-Wülckow, pp. 60–61.

28.
Le Corbusier, *Towards a New Architecture*, 1927, p. 38.
29.
Ibid., p. 19.
30.
Ibid., p. 18.
31.
The letter from Le Corbusier to Gropius asking for the loan of these illustrations is in the Archive Le Corbusier in Paris; and in his eulogy after Le Corbusier's death, Gropius specifically mentioned that he had given him illustrations of grain silos.
32.
Turner, *The Education of Le Corbusier*, 1977, p. 81 and figs. 30, 31.
33.
Le Corbusier, p. 30.
34.
Ibid., p. 29.
35.
Ibid., p. 27.
36.
Ibid., p. 31.
37.
Plato, "Philebus," in *The Collected Dialogues of Plato*, edited by Hamilton and Cairns, 1961, p. 1132.
38.
Le Corbusier, p. 33.
39.
Ibid., pp. 37–39.
40.
Worringer, *Abstraktion*, p. 90.
41.
Le Corbusier, pp. 39–40.
42.
Ibid., p. 41.
43.
Ibid., p. 42.
44.
Mumford, *Technics and Civilization*, 1934, illus. 3, facing p. 341.
45.
Behrendt, *Modern Building*, 1937, p. 99.
46.
Ginzburg, *Stil'i epokha.* English translation by Anatole Senkevitch, Jr. as *Style and Epoch*, 1982, p. 46.

47.
Ibid., p. 70.
48.
Ibid., p. 93.
49.
Ibid., p. 108.
50.
Ibid., p. 109.
51.
de'Seta, *La Cultura Architettonica in Italia fra le Due Guerre*, 1972, p. 182.
52.
Agnelli had been in Detroit and had there met Henry Ford, apparently. If he was already thinking of a new factory, consultation with the Kahn office seems probable, but the generality of the detailing at Lingotto looks more like that of Lockwood, Greene and Co. of Boston.
53.
The account of the building of Lingotto given here is derived largely from conversations with Maria Grazia Dapra Conti, from her book *Visite al Lingotto* of 1984, and Antonello Negri's chapter in *Archaeologia Industriale* (in the TCI series "Italia Meravigliosa"), edited by Rosella Bigi, 1983.
54.
On this, see, for instance, Griff Borgeson, *The Golden Age of the American Racing Car*, 1966, pp. 25–31.
55.
Marinetti, *Manifesto Futurista dell'Architettura Aerea*, 1934, as quoted in Conti.
56.
Negri, in *Archaeologia Industriale*, p. 65.
57.
See the account given in Veronesi, *Difficoltà Politiche dell'Architettura Moderna in Italia 1920–1940*, 1953, p. 119.
58.
Edoardo Persico, Tutte le Opere, 1923–1935, edited by Giulia Veronesi, 1964, vol. II, pp. 311–312. Author's translation.
59.
Ibid., pp. 3–5. Author's translation.

Index

Aberthaw Construction Company
  (Boston), 87, 89–90
Abstraktion und Einfuhlung (Wor-
  ringer), 197, 204, 258n, 259n
Agyptische Kunst (Worringer). *See
  Egyptian Art*
Agnelli, Giovanni, 179, 237, 239
Akron, Ohio (Quaker Square), 175
Alameda, California, 35
Alberti, Leon Battista (*De Re
  Aedificatoria*), 233
Alfeld-an-der-Leine, 11, 181, 185
Allgemeine Elektrizitäts Gesellschaft
  (AEG), 72, 186, 200, 201
Alling and Corry
  Buffalo, 99, 101
  Cincinnati, 14, 101, 211
American Architect and Building News,
  22, 59, 62, 256n
American Architecture and Urbanism
  (Scully), 15, 255n
American Building Art (Condit), 34
Amerika: Bilderbuch eines Architekten
  (Mendelsohn), 144, 230, 257n
Ansaldo (aircraft), 233
Architecture vivante (Morancé), 230
Arctic Oil Company (San Francisco),
  35–36
Atlantis, 8, 9, 21
Atlas Portland Cement Company, 64,
  70, 195, 256n
Austin Company (Cleveland), 179

Bacon, Francis, 8
Bahia Blanca, Argentina (grain
  elevator), 208

Baker, Josephine, 16
Baltimore, Maryland (elevator), 209
Barby an der Elbe (elevator), 213
Barcelona, 107, 175
Barnett-Record System. *See* Johnson-
  Record
Bateman and Johnson, 146
Bauhaus, 3, 7, 11
Bauten der Arbeit und des Werkehrs
  (Müller-Wülckow), 182, 183, 212,
  213, 214
Baxter, A. E., 149, 150, 153, 156, 158,
  160, 167
Bayonne, New Jersey, 64, 65, 72–80,
  106, 107
Behrens, Peter, 72, 184, 186, 187, 194,
  196, 200, 201, 231
Behrent, Walter Curt, 11, 230–231,
  255n, 259n
Belli Arti, Accademia di (Milan), 232
Benevolo, Leonardo (*History of Modern
  Architecture*), 184, 191, 257n
Benscheidt, Carl, 11, 185, 186–187,
  190, 192, 195, 200
Benscheidt, Karl, 185
Berlin Bridge Company, 60
Bethune Hall/Buffalo Meter Company
  (Buffalo), 23, 26–29, 88, 102, 179
Bethune, Louise Blanchard, 23, 45
Beverly, Massachusetts, 11, 68–71, 185
Blauen Bucher, 214
Boccioni, Umberto, 214
Bofill, Ricardo, 175
Borgesen, Griff (*Golden Age of the
  American Racing Car*), 259n

Bottino, Vittorio Bonadé, 239
Bramante, 26–27
  Tempietto, 225, 227
Brick Builder, 257n
Bridgeport, Connecticut, 177
Bronx, the, 60
Brooklyn, 117
Buenos Aires (Bunge y Born elevator),
  12, 207, 219
Buffalo, New York, 5, 6, 10, 19, 20,
  29–30, 39, 82, 89, 107, 154–156,
  168, 169, 171, 225, 233, 242
  Belt Line Railroad, 40, 50, 178
  Bennett Elevator, 112, 113
  City A & B Elevators, 112
  Dakota Elevator, 103, 123, 175,
    177, 207, 223
  grain trade, 154
  Grosvenor & North Division, 44–45
  Perrot Elevator, 155
  Plympton Elevator, 134
  River, 19–20, 114, 165, 175
  State University, 23
Buffalo Veneer Company, 50
Buffalo Weaving and Belt Company,
  37, 40
Buffington, Leroy S., 54, 56
Burchard, Max, 186

Cahiers d'Art, 17, 256n
Calgary, Alberta (Government
  Elevator), 155, 224
Campbell, Joan (*The German Werk-
  bund*), 258n
Cannery Row (Steinbeck), 1, 255n
Cappelen, F. W., 141, 142
Caproni (aircraft), 233
Cary, George, 85, 86, 89
Centre Pompidou (Piano & Rogers),
  165
Chase System, 114, 130
Chiattone, Mario, 11
Chicago, 103, 104, 107
  Schiller Theater, 166
Choisy, Auguste (*Histoire de l'Architec-
  ture*), 217, 222
Cincinnati
  Alling and Corry, 14, 211
  Ingalls Building, 104
  Roth Packing Company, 104, 107,
    211
  United States Printing Co., 210
Cité Industrielle (Garnier), 222
Coalbrookdale, England, 170
Coates, Wells, 232

Concrete Central Elevator (Buffalo),
  156, 164–168, 230
Condit, Carl, 34
Continental Motor Manufacturing Co.
  (Detroit), 13, 103, 195, 196
Copenhagen, 40
Création du monde (Milhaud), 16
Crittall Sash, 242
Crystal Palace (Paxton), 164
Cumbernauld Town Center (Copcutt
  et. al), 165

d'Annunzio, Gabriele, 236
Dapra Conti, Maria Grazia (*Visite al
  Lingotto*), 259n
Dart, Joseph, 110, 111, 123, 130, 173
Daylight Factory, 20, 29, 32, 59, 60,
  62, 63, 72, 74, 106, 109, 177,
  178–179, 193, 236
De Re Aedificatoria (Alberti), 233
Demuth, Charles (*My Egypt*), 205
de'Seta, Cesare, 239 (*La Cultura Ar-
  chitettonica in Italia fra le due
  Guerre*), 259n
Detroit, 7, 107, 171
  Continental Motors, 13, 19, 195,
    196
Deutscher Werkbund, 192, 193, 195,
  196, 198, 199, 201
  Jahrbuch, 11, 97, 146, 195, 200, 230
  Pavilion, 203
Dom-ino (Le Corbusier), 74–75, 216
Domus Aurea (Nero), 157
Duluth, Minnesota, 107
  Great Northern Elevator, 117
  Peavey Elevator, 141–142

Egypt, 6, 19, 136–137, 166, 204–205,
  226
Egyptian Art (Worringer), 108, 197,
  226, 230, 257n, 258n
Electric/Cargill-Electric Elevator (Buffalo), 123–131, 133, 135, 149,
  160, 165, 173–176, 233
Electric Steel Elevator (Minneapolis),
  124
Elzner and Anderson, 104
Engineering News, 60, 104, 118, 132,
  141, 256n, 257n
"Entwicklung der moderner industriebaukunst" (Gropius), 11, 200–
  211, 230, 255n, 257n, 258n
Erie Canal, 110
Esprit Nouveau, 11, 179

Etchells, Frederick, 223
Etlin, Richard, 3, 255n
Evans, Oliver, 110, 243
E-Z Polish plant (Chicago), 89

Faguswerk, 2, 3, 7, 11, 181–194, 200,
    215, 219, 242
Fiat, 179
    Corso Dante, 237
    Lingotto plant, 21, 97, 236–253
    Motori Grandi, 237, 240
"Fireproof Grain Elevators in North
    America," 257n
Fischer Marble Company (Bronx), 60–
    61
Folkwang Museum (Hagen), 195, 196
Ford, Henry, 53, 84, 101, 102, 137,
    232
Ford plant
    Highland Park, Detroit, 7, 84
    New Shop, 90, 97, 171, 178, 237,
        239, 243
    Old Shop, 97, 98, 100–102, 178,
        179, 210, 215, 219, 237, 239
    Picquette Street, 237
    River Rouge, 98, 101, 164, 178, 239
Fort William (elevator at), 12, 206
"Frame of Steel" (Leonard K. Eaton),
    256n
Frankfurt-am-Main (gas works water
    tower), 231
Freyssinet, Eugene, 103, 107, 216
Functional Tradition (Richards), 39

Garnier, Tony (Cité Industrielle), 222
Gaudi, Antoni, 107
German, A.D., warehouse (Richland
    Center), 89
Giedion, Sigfried, 39, 102, 107, 195,
    256n, 258n
    Walter Gropius Work and Teamwork,
        258n
Gilbreth, Frank B., 80
Ginzburg, Moisei, 160, 231–236
    Stil'i epokha, 130, 231–236, 259n
Glasgow, 107
    School of Art, 184
Graphic Controls Inc. (Buffalo), 97,
    169
Great Northern Elevators
    Buffalo, 117–122
    Duluth, 117
    West Superior, 117–118
Great Northern Railway, 117

Gritty Cities (Prokter and Matuzaski),
    177, 246, 257n
Gropius, Walter, 3, 6, 9, 11, 19, 30,
    68, 97, 101, 103, 104, 123, 131,
    136, 144, 146, 148, 153, 160, 164,
    165, 182, 185–191, 195–219,
    222, 227, 230, 236, 255n, 257n,
    258n
Guide to the Industrial Archaeology of
    the Twin Cities, 142

Hadrian's Villa (Tivoli), 157
Haglin, Charles F., 139, 140–141
Haglin-Peavey system, 139–142
Hannover, 11, 185
Hartford (Connecticut), 60
Heidenreich, Lee G., 65, 104, 141
Heffelfinger, Frank T., 137, 140
Heffelfinger, Ruth, 140, 142, 257n
Hennebique, François, 103, 107, 216
Hildebrand, Grant, 101
Histoire de l'Architecture (Choisy), 217,
    222
History of Modern Architecture (Bene-
    volo), 184, 191, 257n
Hitchcock, Henry-Russell, 89, 170,
    256n
Hockanum Mill (Rockville), 80
Hoffman, Josef, 191, 194

Idea dell'Architettura (Lodoli), 28
IIT (Chicago), 27
IMC/St. Anthony 3 Elevator (Min-
    neapolis), 134–136
Industrial Empire of Niagara, 147
Ins Leere Gesprochen (Loos), 258n
International Style, 1, 3, 6, 7, 15, 17,
    18, 21, 107, 184, 242
Iroquois Door and Lumber Company,
    45, 50–51

Jefferson, Thomas, 171
Johnson, Ernest V., 133
Johnson, George H., 117, 133, 138,
    256n
Johnson-Record/Barnett-Record tile
    system, 133–136, 138, 142, 144

Kahn, Albert, 53, 65, 82–87, 90, 96,
    101, 179, 195–196, 232, 237
    and Edward Grey, 98
Kahn, Julius, 65, 86
Kellogg Elevators (Buffalo), 160–162,
    233, 235

Kennedy, John, 132, 257n
Keystone Manufacturing Company
(Buffalo), 61–62, 123
Koestler, Arthur, 31
Kraus (machinery), 233

La Chaux de Fonds, Switzerland, 216
Larkin Company, 39, 102, 178
Administration building, 45–46, 89,
169–170
C building, 59
Chicago Street, 39
L & M warehouse, 47, 48
main plant, 44–45, 178
N Building, 58
R/S/T building/Terminal Warehouse,
88–97, 169
701 Seneca Street, 44–50, 57–59,
90
Learning from Las Vegas (Venturi and
Scott-Brown), 3–4, 6, 255n
Le Corbusier, 3, 6, 7, 8, 11, 15, 23, 26,
28, 29, 30, 74, 84, 102, 103, 136,
142, 153–155, 164, 168, 215–
229, 178, 179, 197, 202, 232,
234, 236, 255n, 256n, 257n, 258n
Legacy of Albert Kahn, 256n
Léger, Fernand, 16
Letters of an Architect (Mendelsohn),
255n
Lockwood, Greene and Co., 31, 85,
86, 87, 88–97
Loos, Adolf, 9, 202, 203, 218–219
Lowell, Massachusetts, 38, 42, 171,
178

Mackintosh, Charles Rennie, 107, 184
Maillart, Robert, 29
Maison Carré (Nîmes), 225
Makepeace, C. R. and Co., 80
Marine A Elevator (Buffalo), 156–160
Marinetti, F. T., 204, 236 (Manifesto
Futurista dell'Architettura Aerea),
259n
Marling, Katharine, 205, 258n
Marseille (Unité d'Habitation), 232
Matté-Trucco, Giacomo, 97, 238–243
Mendelsohn, Erich, 5, 6, 10, 11, 19,
143, 146, 148, 150, 153, 160, 164,
168, 169, 170, 225, 230, 255n,
257n
Meyer, Adolf, 182, 190–191
Milhaud, Darius, 16
Mills College (Oakland), 33

Minneapolis, Minnesota, 29, 54, 107,
130, 134, 168, 171, 172–173,
175, 177
Minterburn/Roosevelt Mill (Rockville),
80–82
Modern Architecture (Taut), 164, 230
Modern Building (Behrendt), 230–231,
259n
Moholy-Nagy, Laszlo, 164, 178, 257n
Monier System, 65, 137, 141
Monol System (Le Corbusier), 216
Monterey, California, 1–2, 5
Monticello, Virginia, 171
Montreal, Quebec, 107, 174
Government Elevator, 103, 164,
206, 219, 223
Marché Bonsecours, 219
Monumentale Kunst und Industriebau
(Gropius), 195–199
Morancé, Albert (Architecture vivante),
230
Morgan, Julia, 33
Mörsch, Ernst, 216
Müller-Wülckow, Walter (Bauten der
Arbeit und des Werkehrs/Blauen
Bucher), 195, 212–214, 258n
Mumford, Lewis (Technics and Civiliza-
tion), 230, 259n
Muthesius, Hermann, 198, 199

Naumann, Friedrich, 11
Negri, Antonello (Archaeologia Indus-
triale), 246, 259n
Newark, New Jersey (Raymond
Boulevard), 42
New Atlantis (Bacon), 8, 255n
New York, 31
Columbia University, 107
Nickel, Richard, 166
Nyhavn (Copenhagen), 40

Ozenfant, Amedée, 179, 257n

Pacific Coast Borax Company
Alameda, 35, 36
Bayonne, 64–65, 72–80, 106
Packard plant (Detroit), 82–83
Building 10, 83–87, 96, 178, 237
Paestum, 166
Paterson, New Jersey, 177
Peavey Elevator (Buffalo), 160, 162,
163
"Peavey's Folly" (Minneapolis), 137–
142, 169, 173

Peavey, Frank H., 140
Percy and Hamilton, 33
Permanence in Building Construction, 256n
Perret, Auguste, 68, 103, 216, 217
Persico, Edoardo, 21, 247, 253 (*Tutte le Opere*), 259n
Pevsner, Nikolaus, 107
Philebus (Plato), 223, 224, 258n
Philadelphia, Pennsylvania, 117
Pierce Arrow plant (Buffalo), 82, 85, 86–88, 89, 178
Pillsbury A Mill (Minneapolis), 54–55
Pillsbury/Great Northern Elevator (Buffalo), 117–123
Pioneer Steel Elevator (Minneapolis), 124, 125, 131
Piranesi, G. B., 56, 166
Piscina Meravigliosa (Baiae), 77
Plato (*Philebus*), 223, 224, 259n
Poelzig, Hans, 201
Pommer, Richard, 256n
Port Costa/"Wheatport," California, 34–35
Prokter and Matuzaski (*Gritty Cities*), 177, 257n
Providence, Rhode Island, 4, 178

Ransome, Ernest L., 11, 32–38, 43, 53, 56, 65–79, 87, 90, 106
  and Smith, 65, 68
  Ransome System, 66–67, 72–80, 87, 88, 104, 169, 185, 239
Raphael (House of), 26
Reidpath, R. J. and Son, 49–50, 52, 54, 57, 96, 101, 123, 144, 153, 160
Reinforced Concrete Buildings (Ransome and Saurbrey), 36, 72, 74
Reinforced Concrete in Factory Construction (Atlas Portland Cement), 36, 64–65, 256n
Richards, J. M., 39
Richardson, H. H., 20
Richland Center, Wisconsin, 89
Riegl, Alois, 197, 205
Riga (Polytechnic), 232
Robinson, D. A., 117
Rockville, Connecticut, 80–82, 171
Roth Packing Company, Cincinnati, 104
Russia, 140, 231–232
Russland, Amerika, Europa (Mendelsohn), 143

Saint Paul, Minnesota, 54
  "Midway," 134, 172
San Francisco
  China Basin, 35
  earthquake, 105
  Golden Gate Park, 33, 168
  Spreckles Building, 228, 229
Sant'Elia, Antonio, 11
Saxony Mill (Rockville), 80
Schindler, R. M., 194
Scully, Vincent, 15, 225, 255n
Selden, George, 137
Sieg des neuen Baustils (Behrendt), 11, 230, 255n
Sheeler, Charles, 164, 178
"Smoketown," 41
Soane, Sir John, 56
South America (corn silo), 13, 208
Space, Time and Architecture (Giedion), 39, 256n
Spengler, Oswald, 232, 233
Spreckles Building (San Francisco), 228, 229
Springfield, Ohio (elevator collapse), 148
Standard Elevator (Buffalo), 116, 156, 158
Standard Oil Company, 74
Stanford, Jane Lathrop, 105
Stanford University, 33, 105
Steinbrenner (ship), 114
Steinbeck, John, 1–2, 255n
Stewart, James and Company, 149
Stil'i epokha (Ginzburg), 130, 232–236, 259n
Stoffregen, Heinz, 201
"Stroikom" (apartments), 232
Sullivan, Louis, 7, 26, 60, 103

Taut, Bruno (*Modern Architecture*), 164, 230
Taylorism, 102
Technics and Civilization (Mumford), 259n
Texas (Panhandle), 142
Toltz, Max, 117, 137
Trier (Basilica), 56
Trotzdem (Loos), 258n
Troy, New York, 170–171
Trussed Concrete Company, 65, 86
Turin (Fiat-Lingotto), 21
Turner, C. A. P., 29, 65, 104, 141
Turner, Paul (*The Education of Le Corbusier*), 219, 259n

United Shoe Machinery Co., 11, 68–71, 75, 82, 123, 185, 187, 190, 239

United States Printing Co. (Cincinnati), 210

Utopia, 8

van der Rohe, Ludwig Mies, 27, 62

Veeder Cyclometer plant (Hartford), 60–61, 62

Venturi, Scott-Brown and Izenour (*Learning from Las Vegas*), 3–4, 255n

Veronesi, Giulia (*Difficolta Politiche dell'Architettura Moderna in Italia*), 259n

Vers une Architecture/Towards a New Architecture (Le Corbusier), 11, 23, 155, 178, 215–229, 232

Von Material zu Architektur (Moholy-Nagy), 164, 257n

Wagner, Martin, 201

Wagner, Otto, 194

Walter Gropius Industriearchitekt (Wilhelm), 203

Walter Gropius und das Faguswerk (Weber), 185, 258n

Washburn-Crosby/General Mills Elevator
  Buffalo, 5, 143–153, 155, 160, 173, 209
  Minneapolis, 209, 233

Washburn Mill (Minneapolis), 54

Waterford, Connecticut, 177

Wayss und Freytag, 137, 195, 212–214, 216

Weber, Helmut (*Walter Gropius und das Faguswerk*), 185, 258n

Weed/McNear warehouse (Port Costa), 34–35

Werner, Edouard, 182, 185–190, 192

West Superior, Wisconsin (Great Northern Elevator), 117

Westbrook, Nicholas, 257n

"Wheatport"/Port Costa, California, 34

Wheat's Ice Cream Company (Buffalo), 52

Wiener Werkstätte, 194

Wilhelm, Karin (*Walter Gropius Industriearchitekt*), 203

Wölfflin, Heinrich, 232, 233

Worms, Germany (elevator), 212

Worringer, Wilhelm, 108, 136, 179, 180, 197, 204–205, 218, 223, 226, 230, 232, 257n, 258n, 259n

Wright, F. L., 20, 45, 54, 89, 103, 107, 169–170, 194, 203
  Wasmuth volumes, 202, 258n